DOCTOR #117641

DOCTOR #117641

A HOLOCAUST MEMOIR

LOUIS J. MICHEELS, M.D.

FOREWORD BY ALBERT J. SOLNIT, M.D.

YALE UNIVERSITY PRESS: NEW HAVEN AND LONDON

Designed by Sally Harris/Summer Hill Books and set in Walbaum and Eras types by Keystone Typesetting, Inc. Printed in the United States of America by Vail-Ballou Press, Binghamton, New York.

Library of Congress Cataloging-in-Publication Data
Micheels, Louis J., 1917–
  Doctor # 117641.
  Bibliography: p.
  1. Holocaust, Jewish (1939–1945)—Netherlands—Personal narratives.
2. Micheels, Louis J., 1917– . 3. Netherlands—Ethnic relations. I. Title.
D804.3.M53 1989   940.53′15′03924   88-27882
ISBN 0-300-04398-8 (alk. paper)

10 9 8 7 6 5 4 3 2 1

This book is dedicated to my wife, my children,
and the memory of my parents and those who did not return

FOREWORD

I have had the privilege of reading successive drafts of this manuscript, and it has been a vital experience. From the first it was clear how essential it is that there be readers for this moving account of human survival in a Nazi death camp, even more than for most books. Readers must join the writer in order to share the reverberations of his profound remembering and to make the telling of his story both complete and unending.

Yet the author could not remember, could not become an active witness to what happened, until he could once again affirm that life is worth living. It took forty years of living after the Holocaust to outbalance the freight Louis Micheels carried from surviving Auschwitz. In *Doctor #117641,* Dr. Micheels uncovers, retrieves, and brings into his "life worth living" the account of his survival of the Holocaust, not only to discharge the burden he has borne for more than four decades, but to demonstrate to others the human tolerance and capacity to survive and transcend a living death through loving and caring for another person. Through their desperately guarded intimacy and privacy and their love for each other, Louis and Nora, his fiancée, safeguarded their grasp on life and humanity as the death forces swirled around them. Alone neither of them could make sense of the world surrounding them, but together they could hold on to the reality of hope, the coherency of enduring, and the vital capacity to be "alone in the presence of others" (Winnicott)—the "others" being the Nazi death camp "guards" who could humiliate them, murder their souls, and snuff out their lives whenever they felt a need to express their murderous, sadistic impulses.

Dr. Micheels is low-key in personality, in writing, and in remembering. Yet his unhistrionic, matter-of-fact style of telling is itself a reassuring demonstration of the patience and indomitability of those who survived and found a way to bring order out of chaos, coherence out of horror, and an affirmation of life out of mass murder.

Psychoanalytic theory and practice have made us aware of the ubiquity of love and aggression, the forces that characterize man's humanity, vitality, and creativity, as well as man's inhumanity to man at its cruelest and most destructive. A child is born relatively helpless and survives because there is usually at least one adult who loves, nurtures, and protects him until he is able to fend for himself. In contrast, aggression can be so little modified by love and tenderness that it leads to destructive acts against others or the self. But aggression may have protective value when it is in the service of hanging on, of struggling against helplessness, and if it has enough self-love and love of others to fuel the struggle against external threats. In fact, there are accounts of recoveries from life-threatening illness or injury that suggest the need for a mix of love of life and aggression in order to survive.

In this book Dr. Micheels tells us how he and his fiancée survived the Holocaust, a man-made catastrophe. Their courtship, which began before the Nazi invasion of the Netherlands, became a lifesaver, the basis for supporting each other after they were imprisoned in the same death camp. Their survival was influenced not only by the realistic skills that a nurse and a medical student could provide in Auschwitz, which made them useful to both their captors and their fellow concentration camp victims, but also by their common reservoir of hope and the ability to borrow strength and adaptive energies from their concern for each other. By helping and loving each other they could endure with determination and a tenacious will to live and not submit to dying. As Martin Buber put it, "Love is responsibility of an I for a Thou."*

The author, with sensitivity and psychoanalytic clarity, describes the limits of endurance and of the human spirit. To some extent the protective functions of aggression in the service of mutual love and caring are evident in this book. But what happens to such a mix of love and aggression once the common enemy, the Nazi threat to life, is vanquished?

Furthermore, the author tactfully questions when and why memory is useful. As a psychoanalyst he is well aware of the costs and burdens of repression. But as a survivor— one who outlasted his oppressors—he knows that the ability to resume a "normal" life after living in a death camp requires a tolerance of forgetting until the resumption of living leads to the capacity to shed the past.

When wondering why Louis Micheels told his story in the 1980s rather than the 1970s or the 1960s, we can only speculate about how much of the unending cycle of life, marriage, parenthood, working successfully, and feeling in charge of one's life is necessary before the right balance is achieved. Besides this very personal question there are other essential ingredients of the inner life that must be available in order to recall and share this life experience. As Rabbi Hillel said, "If I am not for myself, who is for me? And if I am only for myself, what am I? And if not now, when?"**

This book comes as a reminder of the Holocaust at a time when man's inhumanity to man is on the rise. In the

---

*Aleuf Hareven suggested the use of this quotation here, in Jerusalem in 1988.
**Pirke Avot (Ethics of the Fathers) 1:14.

past thirty years there have been civil wars, terrorist outbreaks, and incredibly brutal killings, the most recent of which (the Iraq-Iran War) has led to the loss of over a million lives. We need to remember in order to limit and prevent such unacceptable, inhuman group behaviors, of which genocide as state policy is the most brutal and depraved. At a time when nuclear energy can be a pathway to world destruction or to world conservation, successive waves of remembering are necessary, especially by those who have survived after witnessing. This may be the last wave of such direct observational experiences of the Holocaust.

Like racial prejudice, man's capacity for inhumanity cannot be eliminated; it can only be assumed to be a basic potential of the human animal that may bring about the worst brutality, genocide, a repetition of the Holocaust. Yet this same potential can lead to altruism, camaraderie, and working and living together in peace.

How to remind all of us effectively that the basic ingredients that constitute the human animal have the potential for anticivilization or for procivilization is a profound issue. The obstacles to knowing this are always changing, and in their complexity over time they become devilishly disguised in subtle, unexpected, or unpredictable ways, especially in the guise of nationalism.

This book by Louis Micheels is at least as important in reminding us of our capacity for anticivilization and destructiveness as it is in its own right. And its own importance includes why it takes so long to remember what happened, for one person to pass on to us his love of life in the context of the Holocaust. At the outset—and the author is aware of this—the recollections cannot be complete and cannot be error-free; but they can be and are coherent, and they bring the past and present together in a personal way that yields valid lessons about the Holocaust, about Auschwitz, and about how important love is for survival. We have a regrettable tendency to be led more easily to hatred and bestiality than to love. Doctor Micheels's recollections demonstrate how the demands of the human condition can tap into and extract from the inner life of the individual what is needed and what will serve in a death camp. This includes his own need to wait for forty years of healing and life-validating experiences before he was able to write so that others could join him in witnessing and, one hopes, in preventing another Holocaust. For him this book becomes a formal declaration of his "love of light and determination to trace the moral chain of his being."*

Albert J. Solnit, M.D.

---

*Scott Donaldson, *John Cheever: A Biography* (New York: Random House, 1988).

ACKNOWLEDGMENTS

I want to thank all those friends and family who made it possible for me to write this book. Some were particularly instrumental in my becoming involved in the process of remembering. Ann Rose was the first to lead me to this work; then others, such as Dori Laub and especially Sydney Kramer, nudged me on. Robert Lifton was important in persuading me that my story should be published. Yet if it were not for Al Solnit's understanding and persistent support this memoir might not have been put in print. Equally important were those who not only helped to put the manuscript into a presentable form but also made this work a pleasurable and exciting task—Jean Steinberg, then Gladys Topkis and Stacey Mandelbaum, who with their insight and encouragement helped to put the book in its final shape.

PROLOGUE

In early May 1982 I set foot on German soil for the first time in thirty-seven years. My wife and I were on our way to retrace my journey from Dachau to the Austrian border at the end of April 1945, just before the liberation of the camp by the American army.

It was drizzling when we touched ground at the Munich airport. The buildings were uncrowded; it was Sunday morning, and we passed the usual controls quite rapidly. This helped to set my mind at ease and lessen my apprehension about actually intruding into the past. The girl at the car-rental booth, the first German we spoke with, was very pleasant and efficient. I found that my long-dormant knowledge of German was there when I needed it, without too much difficulty. She explained how to get to Garmisch-Partenkirchen and to Mittenwald, our destination for the first day. It was in the latter town that I had experienced my first days of freedom after a harrowing escape.

The more I had reimmersed myself in my concentration camp experiences while writing this book, the more I felt the need to revisit the actual site of one of the most momentous episodes of my life, previously almost forgotten. It was as if I needed to make certain that it all had happened and leave it behind. At the same time I felt almost a nostalgia for the place where my deepest wish—to survive the Holocaust—had come true, where I had had my moment of victory over the murderous oppressor.

We drove through the outskirts of Munich, making good time in the light traffic. As soon as we left the city behind us the countryside began to look familiar. I had seen the same green fields with patches of pine groves and neat farmhouses when we left Dachau in a transport by train late in April 1945. I told my wife to expect the gentle sloping hills to get steeper as we proceeded southward.

In 1945 I had had no idea where we were going. We had heard rumors about Innsbruck and the Tirol. The Nazis had had some notion of establishing a national redoubt in the Tirolian Alps; perhaps they wanted to use us, all six hundred of us, as hostages. We had become convinced, more than ever before, that we had to escape. The countryside that day had looked so peaceful and neatly cultivated, the houses and villages so picturesque, and the people so unaware of that train with its unusual passengers.

Now the hills were becoming snow-covered peaks, partly hidden in the clouds. The lower fields had a contrasting deep green color, providing a setting that seemed totally unrelated to my concerns. I felt more and more curious and apprehensive about what we would find on reaching Mittenwald. I thought of what we had planned after this "return to the past"—of the friends and relatives in Holland with whom we would spend a week in my old hometown—as if Mittenwald were already behind us.

As we approached the little town, twenty minutes later, I was amazed to see the military barracks where I had spent two weeks helping to organize a clinic in what was to be a displaced persons camp. Now the German army was using the barracks again. At a large gas station on the main street I asked directions to our hotel. I was struck by the attendant's friendliness. Would he have acted the same way if I had told him that I had been there in 1945 as a survivor of the camps? I did not test him.

My wife and I soon found our way, with the help of some signs, to the small hotel on a high meadow overlooking the town. The woman at the desk was very pleasant and gave us a beautiful room with a large balcony and a view of Mittenwald. Again it was on my lips to tell her, "I was here thirty-seven years ago under very different circumstances" to see her reaction. I could not rid myself of the sense that if she knew I had been in a concentration camp and was Jewish we would not have received the same friendly welcome. Although I realized that these feelings were probably unfounded, I chose to pass as an ordinary tourist and could not let down my guard completely.

After lunch we explored the town and its surroundings. First we went to look at the area to the south, where the main road runs along the Isar and the railroad toward Scharnitz on the border with Austria. The Karwendel mountain range to our left, the slopes covered with spruce, were all there as on the day I escaped into those woods. The dry pebble beach in a bend of the river seemed identical to the place where my companions and I had been rounded up for annihilation. Even the gully near the riverbank still existed as when I had tried to hide from Nazi bullets, hugging the ground and wrapped in a snow-covered blanket for camouflage. I showed my wife the little log cabin used to store hay where I had slept away my first hour of temporary freedom, until retreating German soldiers took me prisoner again. I saw the steep stone slides high up near the tree line where I had sneaked across loosening boulders, terrified that the Nazis would spot me again. We found the very section of the road where I had met the spearhead of the American Seventh Army, the G.I.'s on their tanks and jeeps who really gave us our freedom back and told us any house in Mittenwald was ours. The chalet overlooking the southern approach to the village, where I had first tasted again the "luxuries" of normal life, stood where I had left it all those years ago. It had been remodeled into an apartment building. Karl's name was not among those in the directory; apparently he and his family did not live there anymore. I felt as if I had been there just yesterday and wondered what had happened to the three fellow survivors who had stayed with me in that house. I hoped that I might see one of them, Ellis, in Holland.

By now I felt more secure in my exploration of this place. I even looked in the phone book to see whether there was a listing for Münch, who had been an S.S. doctor in Auschwitz, the only one who had been consistently helpful to prisoners. When I learned that he was practicing medicine not far from Mittenwald, I toyed with the idea of getting in touch with him. There were, however, many people with that name in the phone book and no indication that any of them was a doctor, so I gave up. Later on in Holland, Ellis reminded me that shortly before we were shipped out of Dachau Münch had given us a map to help us find his home in case we escaped. Ellis also surprised me with the news that he had met Münch a year earlier when he, the ex-prisoner, and Münch, the former S.S. doctor, discussed their concentration camp experiences on a German television show.

The apprehension that I experienced approaching Mittenwald was clearly related to my "return" to my life in the prison camps of the Third Reich. My fear of blurring the boundary between past and present was an important factor in the delay of writing this book. To unlock the gate to that part of my life took a long time. When I began to write, however, memory came relatively easily and, insofar as I have been able to check, with reasonable accuracy. Writing this work, fortunately, has caused me less emotional upheaval than I might have expected and has even resulted in an important widening of my horizon. I hope it will do the same for the reader.

I have used pseudonyms for some of the persons mentioned in this book to protect their privacy. I did the same with those whose true names escaped my memory.

It was spring 1940, one of those rare times in Holland when the air is mild, pleasantly warm. The shade trees were turning bright green, fruit trees were in bloom, and the sky was blue and clear. Exam time was drawing near, putting an end to the basic-science and theoretical portion of my medical training. I had been studying very hard and had paid little heed to the outside world, including the rumors of a possible German invasion of Holland. I had developed a sort of protective shell, an indifference toward anything that might interfere with my studies. And so, on the evening of 9 May I fell into bed exhausted, only to be awakened around 4 A.M. by the noise of antiaircraft guns.

This in itself was not unusual. The Dutch fired warning shots at planes flying over Holland on their way to or from England and Germany. But no planes were ever hit; hurting or killing people was not part of the Dutch nature. Having stayed neutral in World War I, they had settled into a relatively peaceful routine. Compared with life in other parts of the world, theirs was one of moderation and tolerance. Hitting aircraft did not fit into that scheme.

This time, however, the shooting did not stop at a warning; it continued. I turned over in bed and tried unsuccessfully to get back to sleep. Finally I got up and looked out the window. In the early dawn I saw several formations of low-flying trimotor Junker aircraft and realized with a sinking feeling that the "Huns" had come, parachutists and all. I dressed in a hurry and ran out on the street to a newspaper office. There I read a bulletin that Germany had invaded the Netherlands, that there was heavy ground fighting in the east, and that paratroops had landed behind the main lines of fortification. The Rotterdam airfield and others were being bombed. Our worst fears had become reality. My life, the life of my family, of everyone I knew, and our whole country were in grave danger. The unthinkable had come to pass.

I had grown up in Bloemendaal, a small village eighteen miles west of Amsterdam. The population comprised several "old" families with large estates stretching from the coast through the dunes to the inland woods and meadows; a core of tradespeople, store owners, going back several generations; and a group of commuters to Amsterdam, mostly business people, some professionals, and a few artists—a picture of quiet prosperity. If one could look upon Holland as a whole as a haven from a strifetorn world, Bloemendaal in particular represented an enclave where I had been shielded from most forms of physical or emotional deprivation. Even today this village, nestled in the woods between the dunes and the fields of the lowlands, has preserved itself in the age of the expressway and megalopolis. Most of the houses, open spaces, and roads have remained undisturbed. So, indeed, the events of that early morning shook the very foundation of my life.

Planes continued to fly over Utrecht, where I was attending medical school. I ran back to my room and woke my friend Anton, who lived in the same house. Anton was a tall, thin, wiry young man with plain, open features. His background was very similar to mine, and we had a great deal in common. My father was a stockbroker, his an executive in a large food-packaging company. His family had a summer house near my parents' home. The main concern of both our mothers was the well-being of their family.

Anton's mother wrote books on women's issues and family life. Both families were close-knit, interested in the arts, history, economics, and political issues, also in exploring our country and the Continent by foot, bicycle, and train.

Anton and I had occasionally talked about how, if the worst were to come, we would escape to England. We had never even mentioned the fact that I was Jewish and Anton wasn't, but suddenly that fact loomed large: my life was in greater danger than his. I felt as if suddenly I was totally exposed to a pernicious and evil force. Anton, who did not share this immediate sense of danger—of being categorized as an inferior, an unwanted, dangerous person without any recourse to law—was more curious about the future and could afford to postpone a decision. He thought he'd stay in Utrecht, at least for a while, and fight within the framework of the university and its social setting, but I decided to make a run for freedom.

No cars were available, so I climbed on my bicycle, my most essential belongings tied to the rack, and took off for Bloemendaal. The roads were empty, the sun was shining, the cattle were grazing on the meadows along the river Vecht—a peaceful setting except for the small groups of soldiers dug in around bridges or behind dikes and the occasional bursts of antiaircraft fire. These contrasts only served to emphasize my sense of tragedy. No past experience, either personal or vicarious, had prepared me for this. Full of bewildering feelings and thoughts, I reached Amsterdam in no time. I stopped at my father's office only to learn that he had gone to the British consulate to inquire about the chances of getting aboard a ship to England.

I continued on my way. When I arrived in Bloemendaal I was greeted by an unexpected sight. This small town had not changed in the twenty-three years I had known it; to me it represented the epitome of stability and security. How could it have been transformed almost overnight? The places I had passed on my way to school and on walks with my father now were manned by soldiers shooting at airplanes and searching for parachutists, many of whom were disguised as civilians. Some of the enemy soldiers were women, many of them Germans who until recently had worked for Dutch families as domestics. We, too, had had German domestic help. What if I were taken for a paratrooper? How could they know? But I got home safely, and my father returned shortly thereafter. He told us that one or two passenger ships might be leaving for England, but he seemed reluctant to get out immediately.

My mother, as usual in an emergency, remained calm, perhaps too calm. She prepared lunch and left the speculation and decisions to my father and me. But her eyes betrayed her feelings, a mixture of worry and, to me, disturbing resignation. We turned on the radio. Rotterdam had been bombed. The oil depots were burning out of control. People were fleeing in droves to Belgium and France. There were rumors that Amsterdam would be bombed too. Members of the Nationale Socialistische Beweging, or NSB—Dutch Nazis—were being rounded up and arrested. The queen, accompanied by members of her government, was preparing to leave for England. I went to the local civil defense office, where I was made a medical assistant and given an identifying armband.

Memories of the remote and near past floated through my mind: my childhood, on the whole a good time; the Depression, adolescence, and high school, a period not without turmoil and anxieties. Then came medical school and student life, a carefree time with new friends, both men and women, relative independence, and successes—a time of proving myself, of a profound lust for life. What was going to happen now? The storm clouds looked very dark indeed, even though the sun was shining brightly and spring was bursting out all over.

My secondary education in Het Stedelijk Gymnasium in Haarlem had coincided with the Great Depression and with Hitler's rise to power. By 1934 we were aware of his rantings, his anti-Semitic racist ravings. All this was foreign to the Dutch nature and the tradition of harboring victims of religious or political persecution, and no one thought anything like the Nazi takeover could happen in Holland. Yet certain incidents should have served as a warning, if one had only dared to look. Some of our teachers, three out of about twenty, were obviously leaning toward national socialism; two were members of the NSB. None, of course, was openly anti-Semitic. Besides the NSB there was a Dutch Nazi party modeled on the German party. The daughter of the Dutch "führer" happened to be in my class. She wore a swastika lapel insignia. One day in 1933, the principal of our school uncharacteristically burst into our classroom, interrupting our Latin class. He walked to the front of the room, the offensive swastika insignia in his raised right hand. Enraged, he shouted, "Who in this class dares to wear this obscene symbol of hatred?" There was dead silence. Everybody knew who the culprit was. Nobody had ever seen our calm yet strong-minded principal in such a state. After what seemed an eternity, the culprit, usually very inconspicuous and somewhat shy, raised her hand. Like an expert pitcher the principal hurled the button across the classroom toward the rear corner where she was sitting, just missing her, and announced that he would not tolerate any such display of political provocation in our school. There was profound silence; all of us suddenly became aware of the far-reaching significance of this incident. Yet, though I never forgot the frightening nature of the foreign intrusion, after a while I put it aside with other such warnings.

The Greek teacher we had a year or two later was typical of people apparently receptive to Nazi propaganda. He was a rather volatile, eccentric, unpredictable man who occasionally even had physical fights with students. I once got into trouble with him over an old edition of Homer's *Odyssey* that had a Latin version alongside the Greek text. He knew that I had it, and when I wrote a very good translation of a section in the text he accused me of using the Latin translation to help me with the possibly less familiar Greek. He made me take the test over again, this time using a copy with only the Greek text. Fortunately I again did well, after which he asked me to sell him the old book, a collector's item. I refused. That book is still in my library. He was jealous of others and envious of their possessions. People like him, uncertain of their identity and the limits of their role, were attracted to the oversimplified, concrete, and radical nature of the Nazi ideology, which he claimed would excise the "cancer" from our society. By cancer he meant people more successful than himself, particularly Jews. Having to deal with people like these in and out of school made adolescence a trying period for me, an anxious time in which I came face to face with a real danger: the threatened loss of our cherished way of life.

I thrived on sports and found working with my body a welcome relief from the demands of school. It gave me a certain toughness and hardiness, and these proved of great value later on in my struggle for survival. Fortunately, while a student at the University of Utrecht I made some very close friends, such as Anton, and found a solidarity that turned my medical school experience into one of the best times of my life.

Ellis, an advanced medical student about six years my senior and a fellow member of Het Utrechtsch Studenten Corps, the major student organization, had become a good friend in my first year at the university. As an older student he had been helpful to me, and although we rarely talked about it, the fact that both of us were Jewish made for a special bond in a student organization whose Jewish members could be counted on the fingers of one hand. He was energetic, enterprising, a perfectionist, and not only intensely interested in bacteriology but enthusiastic about sailing. In the summer after my first year we had camped and sailed around the Norfolk Broads in eastern England.

In the winter of 1938 Ellis introduced me to a Zionist student group that organized weekend meetings a couple of times a year to discuss the Jewish problem and the Zionist solution. Although I was aware of and interested in Zionism, it was not until the advent of Hitler that I began to see it as pertinent to my social environment rather than largely an abstraction. The discussions we carried on were of a highly philosophical nature and gave me at least a sense of doing something about this increasingly acute and potentially explosive issue.

It was at such a weekend meeting in the autumn of 1939, after the Dutch army had been mobilized, that I met Nora. To me she seemed different from the other women there, more interested in the problems we were discussing yet also very feminine, with a concerned expression in her almond-shaped, light gray eyes. Her slightly prominent cheekbones and straight black hair gave her a strangely Oriental look. She was simply dressed in dark slacks with a red sweater over a white blouse. Soon I found we were sitting near or next to each other during the various discussion sessions. We each managed to make it look accidental until we realized we were both doing it and that the attraction was mutual. After that we became quite explicit.

Nora, a music student in a well-known school in Amsterdam, played both the flute and piano. I also met her older brother, Bernard, a medical student, at the meeting. She had a younger brother, Bob, who played the cello. Her father was a physician, a general practitioner in Amsterdam. We talked about my family—my sister, Els, the eldest, who was living in England, and my brother, Lex, also older than I, in the Dutch army. We agreed that we should follow my sister's example and move to either England or Israel, then still called Palestine. Such ideas turned out to be, regrettably, wishful thinking rather than serious plans. As a matter of fact, I had returned from a visit to Els and her husband and infant son the day before Germany invaded Poland.

Nora and I continued to see and write each other regularly. We discovered that our parents were acquainted. Our relationship, which rapidly turned into a romantic one, became vitally important to both of us in the face of an increasingly threatening world. Nora gave me a sense of stability and responsibility and added a new dimension of intimacy and ambition to my life. The relationship marked the end of my adolescence. When a ticket clerk in the railroad station addressed me as "young man" I felt insulted.

The immediate turmoil of the invasion had subsided somewhat, but the outcome was obvious after four days. Most of the defense lines coordinated with inundations were rendered useless by the enemy's massive employment of paratroops and by betrayal and sabotage by the fifth column. My family had learned that our best chance of escape was to go to IJmuiden and there board a ship, either civilian or military, for England. I managed to rent a car, an old Model T, and my father, mother, and I packed a few of our belongings, our "escape bag." During the fifteen-mile ride we had to stop several times because of heavy explosions near IJmuiden. It was a road with many turns, and I was driving as fast as I could. Inadvertently I added to the excitement by not realizing how tippy the old buggy was. At some of the curves it felt as if the car would roll over, but I managed to keep it upright. This part of the ride, with the explosions and our frantic need to escape, would have been like a kind of Wild West movie if it had not been so terrifyingly real. We were not sure whether the Germans were bombing the port or our countrymen were blowing up installations to make them useless for the Germans. As we came closer, we met many acquaintances, all trying to find a means of escape.

In Velsen, in a park near the port, we seemed literally and figuratively to have come to the end of the road. There was a mass of people, almost all of them Jews, from all over the country—Amsterdam, Utrecht, The Hague, Haarlem. I don't believe I had ever seen so many Jews in one place, all desperately trying to get out at the last minute, aware of the heavy odds against succeeding. The British consul was in a pavilion surrounded by thousands of people begging for one of the handful of available places on a destroyer. There were also some fishing trawlers whose captains did a booming business transporting people for large sums of money. A business friend of my father knew of a fishing boat that had room for one more person. I decided that unless all of us could go I would not go either. Finally, like most of the others, we chose to return home and try again early the next morning. It suddenly dawned on me that we had left everything behind: home, possessions, relatives, friends, including Nora, to make this desperate effort.

To our surprise, when we reached home we were welcomed by Nora and her parents. They had left Amsterdam, fearing the threatened bombing if Holland did not surrender. They also had had some idea of going to IJmuiden but rightly assumed that chances of getting out were not very good. The idea of uprooting ourselves, leaving everything and everybody behind, not the least our country, and my own mixed feelings about escaping, were numbing and perplexing.

We all sat down to dinner at our house, trying to deny all that was happening. The news that evening confirmed rumors that Holland had surrendered to the Nazis, and the population was advised to go back to work and return to routine. "No cause for alarm. If you are a law-abiding citizen no harm will come to you." Nora's parents temporarily moved into a beautiful house belonging to an uncle and aunt of mine who had left for the United States in September 1939 and had put my father in charge of their affairs. Nora stayed in our house for the first time.

When I awoke very early next morning it came to me that we were in Nazi-occupied territory, and I was overcome with loathing and fear. Nora was staying in my room, and I slept in a spare bedroom in the attic, conforming to the customs and expectations of our parents. It did not take me long, however, to get up and go downstairs to Nora. She was not at all surprised; she had not slept well herself and had been expecting me. It was the first time we made love. We said little, holding onto each other very tightly, as though wanting to hide in each other's arms. Although the thought crossed my mind, I did not say that if we wanted to make another attempt at escaping to England we ought to leave right away. Nora did not say anything, and my parents did not stir either. Our new engulfing sense of closeness, enjoyment, and reassurance overrode any ominous but realistic considerations, such as the general assumption that if the Nazis came the Jews would be done for. Yet another worry stopped me from actively pursuing the escape to England, namely, that German troops or the navy might already have occupied IJmuiden and the coastal waters and might take us prisoners.

All these notions receded rapidly, and I began to look forward with a false kind of optimism toward a new phase in my life with Nora, in which we would savor the beautiful spring and possibly take a brief vacation before resuming our normal lives. Everybody seemed automatically to have joined in the same sort of conspiracy, fueled by a strange but powerful inertia, a need to stick with our known, proven, safe way of life. Our escape plan fizzled, replaced by this new intimacy between Nora and me. But for a long time, after the temporary relief of peaceful sleep, I would wake up early with a feeling of doom hanging over me like a heavy, suffocating blanket.

Once the mayor of Bloemendaal, standing in front of the town hall, had announced the official surrender, the deep gloom, the warlike atmosphere, the soldiers manning guns, the airplanes and shooting disappeared as if by magic. Stores reopened, and people went about their affairs as if nothing had changed. I took my bike and rode to see Anton, who was spending the weekend at his family's summer home in Santpoort. His parents, especially his mother, were deeply worried, yet thankful that the queen, symbol of Holland's freedom, had escaped to England. We thought about what the future might hold in store, but our immediate concerns, such as gasoline and food, were of a more prosaic nature. We predicted quite accurately that driving would soon be a thing of the past. Most of the oil tanks in Rotterdam had been blown up, and whatever gas was left was sure to be confiscated by the Germans. Rumors abounded, but the newspapers sought to reassure us that nothing was going to change. The occupation of Holland would be a purely military affair, nothing more. The population was asked to remain calm and law-abiding and to refrain from furnishing any pretext for reprisals. It did not take long, however, for the NSB to surface, some members wearing only insignia, others boldly in black uniforms and jackboots, and for the German army to march through the streets singing their Nazi songs. From the very beginning, the people ignored them; this was to prove one of the greatest frustrations for the Germans in their dealings with the Dutch. Like most others, my parents settled back into their routine, getting together with friends, discussing events over a drink, a cup of tea, or a game of cards. My mother, as usual, directed her energies toward family and home, making sure that our larder was well stocked and keeping in touch with friends. She could be outspoken and stubborn once she made up her mind and was more inclined to worry than my father. He was more volatile and showed his feelings and moods more readily. I could always tell the minute he came home from his office what kind of day he had had. When in a good mood, which was more often than not, he was a tremendously stimulating and invigorating presence. Under his influence a kind of forced optimism and a sense of togetherness in the face of the enemy took hold.

Nora's parents were part of our circle of friends, and Nora and I spent much time together, walking in the dunes, enjoying the burgeoning spring, the flowers, the smell of jasmine, the countryside. I introduced Nora to my favorite walks through dunes known to only a few others. We drank in the peaceful atmosphere as if fearing that it all might be taken away from us soon.

Hitler and anti-Semitism were never discussed. We clung to our ingrained tendency to deny the obvious; a false, unreal sense of security took over. We had more time to wonder what had become of my brother, Lex, and his wife, who had gone to Paris in April, just before the invasion. An uncle and aunt were there, too. It felt eerie to suddenly have lost contact with them. We assumed, as later proved correct, that they had joined forces and fled south to Spain.

In the first few weeks after the surrender a number of our friends and acquaintances disappeared. Some, we assumed, had managed to get to England or France, but many, in some cases whole families, had committed suicide. Such grim news, however, was quickly compartmentalized and stored away. It was not to be discussed. Father went back to his office, where activity of sorts continued. Mother resumed her work in the house, and I returned to Utrecht and studied as hard as I could for my candidate's midway exam in June.

I had the use of a sailboat belonging to a cousin who had left for the United States about six months earlier, and after I passed my exam, Anton, another medical student named Rens, and I embarked on our customary trip through the canals and lakes, from Utrecht to western Holland to some lakes not far from our home. About halfway along we got hold of a newspaper—portable radios did not then exist—and learned that regulations were being prepared which would exclude Jews from public places, theaters, restaurants, and parks. Although these laws were allegedly not as rigid as the so-called Nuremberg Laws and had not yet been enacted, the announcement had a devastating effect on me, rekindling that hovering sense of doom.

I told Anton and Rens how good I had been feeling about passing my exam and embarking on the clinical part of my medical training and about being able to relax on our sailboat until this Nazi monster had reared its head again. Anton sought to reassure me, saying that things probably wouldn't get as ugly as I feared. And so we continued on our trip, and I managed gradually to push my fears aside.

During that summer of 1940, a friend introduced me to the person with whom I had my first real job, a farmer in the Wieringer Meer. A native of Zeeland, hardworking, enterprising, devoutly religious, patriotic, he was one of the first settlers in this part of the reclaimed Zuiderzee. Even though he could not understand why a medical student would want to spend part of a summer vacation working with him, he could understand that it felt good to be away from the outside world for a month, to return to the very basics of life, to grow what you eat, to be close to the soil and do hard physical work. In retrospect, it was as if I knew I had to get in shape, literally and figuratively, for what lay ahead. It was hard work indeed, getting up with sunrise about 5 A.M. and hitting the sack at 9 P.M., exhausted, but I never ate as much or felt as good.

IV

In the fall of 1940 it became clear that Holland was going to be annexed by the Third Reich and put under civilian rule, with Arthur Seyss-Inquart as the führer. Before long he was being compared with the Duke of Alba, who in the sixteenth century, during the Spanish occupation, had ruled and oppressed Holland. And the two were indeed equally cruel. The Dutch habit of treating the Germans as if they were air, invisible, brushing by them on the streets, writing slogans like "Orange on top" on walls, the underground activity and sabotage—this drove the Germans mad. Their propaganda simply wasn't as effective in Holland as in most other countries. In Belgium and France the Nazis apparently were having an easier time. There people either were more willing to bargain and trade or they fought them directly. Consequently, German rule in those countries never became quite as extreme as in Holland. Their military governments were less concerned with political goals and racial policies, and deportations of Jews were not as rampant.* In Holland, in spring 1941, the Nazis began to bar Jews from participating in the performing arts in public theaters and

*In France one-third of all Jews were deported, in Belgium, one-half, and in Holland, three-quarters (Milton Dank, *The French Against the French* [Philadelphia and New York: Lippincott, 1974]; Hannah Arendt, *Eichmann in Jerusalem* [New York: Viking, 1964]).

orchestras. Restaurants were ordered to post signs "Joden niet gewenst" (Jews not welcome). Also toward the end of 1941, the Dutch identity cards of all Jews were stamped with the letter *J*. In their neat and orderly fashion the Dutch had kept meticulous records about everybody and everything. Practically every Jew complied with the order. Slowly but surely the noose was being tightened.

Still, life went on. We even had a meeting of the Zionist Student Organization one weekend, at which some uninvited guests, NSB members, showed up. Fortunately, after some discussion and anxious moments, they left us alone and disappeared. Chamber music recitals by prominent musicians were given in private homes. People, myself among them, resumed long-neglected musical studies and began to play in amateur groups.

The Jewish members of the Amsterdam Concertgebouw formed an orchestra that performed in the Plantage Park Theater, the same building that later, toward the end of 1942, became the detention center for rounded-up Jews before deportation to Westerbork and the death camps. There Nora and I listened to an unforgettably moving performance of the Brahms violin concerto. Whenever I hear it now I can see before me all the many people, like us engrossed in beautiful music, forgetting for the moment the hell outside. The knowledge that this very same place shortly afterward became the stage of one of the most agonizing chapters in the history of mankind remains an excruciatingly painful memory.

In general, however, life at home continued normally, and student life was also going along in routine fashion. I continued my studies and lectures without change in a sort of fatalistic mood, through 1941.

Because of the discrimination in restaurants where we students used to eat fairly regularly, a small group of us began to take our evening meal at the home of an acquaintance whose cooking was good and whose prices were low. He loved to feed us and participate in our discussions about world events, like the war in Africa, speculating whether the British would stop their retreat or whether Tobruk would hold—almost like the World Series, but what a game!

In the summer of 1941, Anton and I went on a trip in a double scull through the canals and rivers in the south of Holland to one of the few wetland areas left. On that trip, in a small bar on 22 June 1941, we heard on the radio that Germany had invaded Russia. This was a high point of our trip. We were convinced that Hitler, by fighting on this vast front, had overreached himself, that he had made a serious miscalculation and would suffer a fate similar to Napoleon's. It also meant, we thought, that he had given up his plan to invade England. The idea of a second front in Western Europe began to take shape.

The weather was beautiful for a change, and the dark clouds in my mind also began to dissipate. Like the work on the farm, this trip, especially the sense of freedom, the closeness to nature in the typically Dutch setting of clouds and water, birds, marshes and canals, made the old Holland more real again, although deeper down I knew that slowly and relentlessly it was slipping away. It felt like the relief a cancer patient probably experiences when a remission sets in—hope against hope that, maybe, everything will yet turn out well. I had been brought up to think this way. Father was a born optimist, and although he was proved right frequently, he was perhaps too trusting, and this eventually led to his and my mother's death.

The ancestors of my parents had settled in the Netherlands toward the end of the eighteenth century. My father's family came from the Cologne area to Maastricht, the capital of the southern province of Limburg. My father was born in Arnhem, where his father worked as an engineer, building railroad bridges. My mother's ancestors came from Germany and settled in Amsterdam around 1800. Her father was a pharmacist. Their way of being Jewish did little or nothing to distinguish them from the gentile Dutch population. Like the majority of Dutch Jews, they were assimilated. At their age, mid-sixties, their way of dealing with catastrophic changes was to dig in and endure. I too found it difficult to see what was obviously coming, to believe that our whole way of life might collapse. My parents, besides having a need to deny the worst, could not adjust to a world in the throes of war and the concomitant change of values, the "each for himself" mentality so foreign to our background.

Separation, violence, and death had been kept away from us. Holland as a whole was known for its moderation. Who would have thought it possible that we would have to scrounge for food as we did once food rationing began in late 1941? Was it not the older generation, with the wisdom of age, who were supposed to be the leaders? They were even more at a loss than the adolescents and young adults like me and my friends.

But on this vacation trip I was able to rekindle my old idealism, so at odds with the war climate, and refuel for the coming battle. Looking back now, some forty years later, I'm not surprised that Anton, my companion on that special vacation, and his family, who to me represented Holland at its best, remained such close friends even though our careers took us to opposite parts of the world.

That same summer, sensing it might be our last chance, Nora and I went on a camping trip to Limburg, searching for respite and finding it in the gentle hills and farms where I had spent my first summer vacation away from home at the age of three. I still remember that summer in 1920 vividly. The village was called Houthem. We lived in a small family hotel, my parents, my sister, Els, six years older than I, my brother, Lex, three years older, and two cousins, Miriam, my sister's age, and Herman, somewhat older than my brother. We children had to sleep in a nearby annex under the supervision of our nursemaid, with whom I felt quite safe. I don't remember feeling anxious about being separated from my parents at night. I had to be careful while playing with the other children because I had burned my left leg below the knee and the wound was healing very slowly. On outings I was often pulled in a cart of a type used for children in those days. Perhaps the special attention I received, but also the many other children with us, made this a very happy time and memory. And now, more than twenty years later, I returned to this idyllic spot, with Nora. Nora shared my love for the outdoors; she was lithe and athletic, a good hiker. We explored the little rivers and brooks and found unusual plants and birds. Nora dug up some flowering plants to take back home for our gardens. We felt that we were in a special sanctuary, safe from the onslaught and the signs of *Juden verboten.* My parents had been apprehensive about our taking a trip while, almost daily, new restrictive edicts against Jews were being issued. But at the farm where we slept in the hayloft, nobody cared whether we were Jews or not.

In general, this was true throughout the countryside. Shortly after our return, however, I again was abruptly confronted with the new reality. I was in Amsterdam in a streetcar on the way to Nora's house. Her father had been forced to hand over most of his medical practice to a non-Jew because Jews were not allowed to treat non-Jews. Because her father's office was in his house, the whole family had to move to an outlying district when his non-Jewish colleague took over. So I had to take a trolley ride of at least twenty minutes from the station to the opposite part of the city. I was lucky to get a seat. Along the way a group of NSB members in their black uniforms and a German girl in army uniform got on the trolley. Ordinarily, men offered their seats to women, but that day nobody did. A little while later one of the NSB members, pointing his finger at me, announced that it was intolerable for a dirty Jew to fail to surrender his seat to a pure Aryan woman. Nobody budged, including me; in keeping with what by now had become a national custom, we all ignored him completely. He shut up, but I was shaken, sick to my stomach, hurt and enraged, though outwardly calm.

I had never before been derided or even teased because I was a Jew. I did not think of myself very much as a Jew, nor did I think that I looked particularly Jewish. But all my old beliefs and feelings were shattered in a matter of seconds. In Bloemendaal most of our friends were not Jewish, and Jews made up fewer than one percent of the total town population. My parents observed the Jewish High Holidays but did not keep a kosher home. I, like my brother, was bar mitzvahed with mixed feelings and without much conviction. The streetcar incident shook me up profoundly and kindled a stubborn determination to survive with an abiding Jewish sense of pride.

V

In February 1941 rumors of deportation began to circulate, especially after a pogrom had failed because of popular resistance. Many non-Jews had beaten up the NSB members and forced them to retreat from the Jewish business sections they had tried to destroy. The *Grüne Polizei*, in retaliation, had rounded up a group of four hundred young Jewish males and deported them to Mauthausen, one of the most notorious concentration camps. Shortly thereafter nearly all were reported dead, among them an acquaintance of mine from the Zionist student group. This was the first instance of such an act of genocide in Holland. The only crime of the victims was being Jews, or as people in Holland tended to say and feel, "being Jewish." No one, including me, grew up with the notion of being *a* Jew, of being part of a race or special group of people. I felt I was Dutch like everybody else, like my friends; my religion, insofar as I was religious, was Jewish. Later I realized how unlike most East European Jews I was in this respect. Even being a Zionist did not mean to me that I was a Jew rather than Jewish. This distinction may seem hair-splitting or inconsequential. But it sheds light on the unbelievable shock that Dutch Jews felt at being discriminated against in a country with this degree of assimilation. This feature of Dutch Jews caused them particular difficulty in dealing with concentration camp life.

Soon the rumor spread that Jewish people over age fifty were going to be rounded up. My feeling of acute helplessness and panic when I learned of this imminent danger to my parents, my efforts to protect them, my frantic consultations with friends about finding a hiding place—all this had an infernal quality that continued, more or less in the background, throughout the war. The rumor turned out to be a false alarm—but would it be the next time? The rumor of a selection of people over fifty held a very ominous meaning. It only confirmed the unthinkable: older people were useless to the Nazis and marked for destruction. I don't know of anybody who actually put this into words. I sensed it, but expressed it only in my frantic activity to protect my parents. I had heard stories of the murder of retarded and mental patients in Germany. If the Germans were capable of that, the annihilation of older people might well be their next move. But one cannot, however, go on for long fully aware of the reality of one's imminent, violent death. At least I could not, and I found myself living in a state of mind where I could make myself forget what I knew the Nazis had in store for people in general and Jews in particular.

After it was mandated in April 1942 that the yellow Star of David be worn on outer garments, some non-Jews offered token resistance by wearing the star on their coats as well. One could fail to wear it, and I did at times, but there was always the risk of being apprehended and asked for identification. False identity cards, without a *J*, became much sought after. The alternative was to be literally an outlaw, an outcast, without any rights whatever. Most Dutch Jews sought protection by the only method they knew, obedience to an authority, which the Nazis provided in the form of the "Joodse Raad," a council composed of prominent Jews. An illusory and dangerous authority indeed! New regulations were issued, labor camps were organized for everybody under the age of fifty, and a special registration in the form of a military draft was instituted. When my turn to register came, a woman friend, a member of the underground, accompanied me to the registration office, and through her intervention my card was destroyed. While I waited she took my card to an office in the back, to someone in the underground who performed this simple but dangerous act. She came back to the waiting area in a few minutes, said "O.K.," and out we went.

This gave me a tremendous lift, far beyond its practical significance. At least something could be done to defend oneself, to fight the enemy, and at all levels of administration and society there were friends ready to risk their own lives to help others.

During the winter of 1941–42 my life at the university, as if by its own momentum, continued more or less as usual, between the shocks of the continued onslaught of new restrictive edicts against Jews, such as having to obtain a special travel permit each time I went from Utrecht to Bloemendaal on weekends. I felt utterly humiliated and angry, and therefore any form of escape from the "rules" brought a sense of relief.

Robert, a chemistry student, was planning to take an important predoctoral exam and was preparing for a party to celebrate his expected success. Liquor could no longer be purchased, so he collected sugar rations from all his invited friends, let the sugar ferment, and, using a home-made rig on his coal-burning stove, distilled this fermented brew into alcohol. When the big day arrived—he had, of course, passed the exam—we had several liters of alcohol on hand. We had managed to obtain various flavoring agents from a plant belonging to relatives who were in the United States and made the most delicious cordials. Everybody attempted to act normally. I do remember one of the guests, not Jewish, commenting how completely exposed and vulnerable anyone wearing the yellow star must feel. So even if for a moment one could forget, it was not for long.

I was beginning to work hard at night to prepare for my doctoral exam, which I planned to take in June 1942. During vacations and weekends I spent considerable time with my parents and Nora. We would go on hikes, make music, talk about people who had escaped and others who had been caught on their way to Switzerland, Spain, or England. Some tugboats or fishing boats managed to make the crossing despite the German guards on board, and their arrival was always broadcast by the BBC. Beach areas were closed off. The Germans were feverishly building bunkers in the dunes all along the coast. Sometimes I would dream about finding an escape route, of getting a small sailboat through the dunes and German lines and sailing to England. These were exciting daydreams, but that was all they were. I think many people became dedicated daydreamers, more inventive or creative than ever before. Perhaps inspired by my fantasies of escaping, I became interested in model boats and built an intricate sailboat model, which I imagined I would sail with my yet unborn children and which I actually took with me on my first trip to the United States after the war as a present for my nephew.

In the spring of 1942 the rumors about young Jews being rounded up became more and more persistent, so much so that for short periods I would hide with non-Jewish friends in Bloemendaal until the danger seemed over, for the moment at least. In Utrecht the situation appeared less tense, perhaps because few Jews lived in the area. Yet some stories began to circulate, frequently from unsophisticated or unreliable sources, that nevertheless proved correct later. I heard from my landlord, an elderly Catholic, that people were being loaded onto trucks and gassed in Poland; others mentioned castration and sterilization. I tended to dismiss such rumors as just that and tried to forget.

I began to keep a diary, which gave me some sense of freedom. It was one place where I could say whatever I felt or thought, an attempt to document the horrible violation of human rights. I wrote in it after our evening meals and hid it in my microscope case, which I left with a non-Jewish friend in the house where we took our evening meal.

New rumors of "inventorization" in Bloemendaal surfaced, and there were actual incidents of Dutch Nazis searching Jewish homes and listing all the valuables, in preparation for stripping Jews of paintings, sculptures, and antiques. We took precautions, hiding many of our valuables with non-Jewish friends and selling others. Earlier the German armed forces, knowing that most middle-class Dutch homes had a great many copper antiques, requisitioned all copperware. We, like almost everybody else, buried most of ours in the dunes. People would jokingly ask, "Is your copper growing yet?"

One night my parents called to say that they had been notified that their home would be inventoried the next day. Shocked, I rushed home to find my mother in great distress but amazingly calm, telling me that my father had been arrested and taken to the police station. A couple of Dutch men in civilian clothes, obviously working for the Nazis, had come early in the morning and taken him away. The most valuable items were gone, so we decorated the house with cheaper substitutes to cover the marks left by the paintings or cabinets formerly there. The searchers had proceeded without many questions until one of them saw my father's bicycle and briefcase in the backyard. They looked in his briefcase and found some business papers and books he had taken home to work on. They thereupon assumed that he was trying to hide highly incriminating papers and took the papers and my father to the police station. When I learned about this I felt that my worst fears had become real. He would be deported to a concentration camp, and we would never see him again.

We did not hear from him all day. I made frantic calls to people I thought might be able to pull some strings to get his release. It looked hopeless. How could my fellow citizens perpetrate such crimes?

Even as a child I had been very sensitive to separations, especially unexpected ones. I remembered how afraid I had been when, during vacation trips to France, my father and brother would get out on the platform at station stops to stretch their legs; I feared that the train would leave without them. I would plead frantically with them to get back on the train before it was too late. Of course, this frequently had the opposite effect; to tease me they would wait until the very last moment, when the conductor would call out, "En voiture!" I used to worry that the conductor would forget to sound this warning.

This time there was really nothing more I could do. I called the police station several times. They were quite friendly, but all they could tell me was that he was all right and talking to the NSB members. Finally, after dark, the front door opened and there he was, all in one piece! Our relief was indescribable. He told us that they had charged him with removing objects before the inventorization and had also questioned him about his office papers. They told him that the firm would be liquidated by the banking firm of Lippman and Rosenthal, which the Nazis had already taken over and which was becoming the repository for all Jewish stockbrokerages, banking firms, and other financial institutions. One of my father's interrogators was a man he knew from the stock exchange. Notably unsuccessful in this business, the man of course blamed the Jews for his misfortune. Yet he was surprisingly benign, and arranged to have my father tell them what he had taken out of the house in exchange for his "freedom." So my father mentioned a few items he had put up for auction and was then let go.

Fortunately, my father had taken enough money out of his firm to provide for us for some time to come, and he was also given a weekly allowance by his Nazi "supervisors." The interrupted inventorization was to be repeated a week later, when the furniture earlier removed by my father was back in place. In the meantime, my parents and I sorted our large collection of family photos and paintings, substituting bad ones for good ones. I made sure to be present on the day of the inventorization, and while the officials were looking around I removed several valuable items from right under their noses, walked out the back door without even my parents' noticing, and took them to friends. I felt the risk was worth it. I had outwitted those thieves and murderers.

This was the prelude to another unbelievable experience in a Western, civilized country. On a specified day and time we had to present ourselves at the railroad station for the official evacuation from Bloemendaal to Amsterdam. No Jews were allowed to live within a certain distance of the North Sea coast, as though the Jews were the only threat to the defense of the shoreline. The real reason clearly was to create a ghetto in Amsterdam, to subject the Jews to greater Nazi control and eventual deportation.

When we presented ourselves with maybe fifteen others at the station on that morning in April 1942, the NSB members checked us while the other travelers looked on. Nobody uttered a word as we boarded the regular train to Amsterdam, leaving Bloemendaal, our home for twenty-four years, behind. All we were allowed to take with us was one suitcase per person. Of course, we had shipped clothes and other daily necessities earlier or stored them temporarily with friends. The enormity of this transfer stunned everybody concerned. What was happening to us right then, that very moment, was unthinkable, and yet it was true, not a bad dream. I cringed to see both my father and mother being dispossessed of everything they had worked for honestly, and above all of their right to live wherever they wished. To see them treated like scum was incomprehensible to everyone who observed this, Jew or non-Jew. My one consoling thought was the conviction that we would be back some day soon.

We had earlier found a rather nice apartment opposite a park in the designated area, next to the botanical garden. After we unpacked and settled down, I returned to Utrecht to continue studying for my doctoral exam.

VI

It felt very strange to be cut off from Bloemendaal, but I did not brood about it. I almost forgot that we had ever lived there, and tried to make Amsterdam my weekend home. Living in Amsterdam brought the advantage of being much closer to Nora, although a new regulation barred Jews from using bicycles or public transportation, so it took me about half an hour to walk to her parents' house. Nora and I had meanwhile announced our official engagement. Actually, we had come to this decision while still in Bloemendaal, during one of our Saturday afternoon walks through the dunes. We had been walking in silence, admiring the beauty of the trees, birds, and soft green moss, when Nora broached the subject.

"We've been seeing each other for two years now, a long time. I feel we know each other well enough to make it more permanent."

"You mean you want to get married?" I said, somewhat surprised.

"Yes—if we know and love and admire each other as we do, why wait?"

"I've thought about us getting married so much that I took it for granted we would, but I felt that under the present circumstance it would be irresponsible. I can't offer you any security, financial or otherwise."

"Oh, Loet, that's really not the point. If anything, I think our present situation is a good reason for making our relationship official."

"I really hadn't looked at it that way," I answered. "But I guess I've been brought up never to be impulsive, not to make promises I can't live up to, always to be careful. I know you're different in this respect, and I admire you for it. I know you're right. Let's tell our parents that we want to get married in the fall."

We were still able to think in terms of continuity, to imagine a stability that allowed for long-term planning. Today this strikes me as rather absurd, but also understandable as one of the many forms of denial without which life would be unbearable.

In Amsterdam, especially, food was becoming scarce; going hungry because there was literally nothing to eat, not merely not enough, was a disturbing experience. I often thought back to my childhood, when my mother had had to coax me to eat something I didn't like. How glad I would have been for it now.

I passed my doctoral exam in June 1942 and managed to get the post of coassistant (intern) at the Nederlands Israelitiesch Ziekenhuis (N.I.Z.) in Amsterdam. This allowed me to live with my parents. Nora, too, had gotten a job there as a practical nurse. Those days in Amsterdam, the specifically Jewish world in and outside the hospital— away from the academic setting, from my student friends, most of whom were not Jewish—was very different from life in Utrecht. Because of the warlike situation, supervision at the hospital was minimal, and I was able to spend much time in the lab doing research I had begun at school, on the effect of vitamin C on the body's defenses against various noxious influences, including tuberculosis. But everything was so unstable and distracting that I seldom had enough consecutive time to make any real progress.

At least once a week somebody from the group I worked with would disappear, either going underground or venturing on the hazardous journey to Switzerland or Spain or being arrested. One of Nora's brothers similarly vanished without a trace. Weeks later we began to fear the worst.

Except for contact with Anton, mostly by phone, I lost touch with the university and Utrecht. Many of my belongings were still in my room; Anton was taking care of them. *Onderduiken* (hiding) or escaping gradually became a more consuming preoccupation. I felt as if this involuntary isolation from many of my friends was a preparation for my disappearance. The fewer people who knew that I had gone into hiding or left the country, the better.

One night in September 1942, after all of us had already gone to bed, the doorbell rang. The house we lived in had three floors and an attic, where I slept. Three families shared this large house. The owners lived on the second floor, and my parents and another elderly couple on the first floor, each in a large room. My parents' room had an enclosed porch with stairs going down into a small yard. My attic room had a window leading out to the roof, which was level with the other roofs on the block. I had been thinking about what I would do in the event of just such a surprise visit. There was a recessed closet, and my first idea had been to hide there. Another possibility was to hide on the roof with the chance of escaping to adjacent houses.

In the event, I went to the top of the stairs. I could not see anything, but I thought I heard a couple of men speaking Dutch. I assumed they must be the Amsterdam police, many of whom by then were Dutch Nazis; most of the non-Nazis had been fired or had resigned. I was wearing pajamas and was ready to hide in my closet. However, I stayed and tried to eavesdrop. The two visitors, my father, and the other husband had apparently gone into the front room on the first floor. I heard their voices faintly; my heart was pounding in my chest. Any moment I expected the Nazis would order everybody out in the street. Both father and I had stamps on our identity cards indicating that we were doing essential work. Would this protect us against deportation? The talking continued, it seemed forever. I moved stealthily down one flight of stairs, but could not hear much more. Finally the door opened. I scrambled back upstairs; the front door closed, and the police were gone. I waited a few minutes before running downstairs. Everybody tried to relax.

"What happened?"

"We paid them twenty-five guilders and told them to spare us a repeat visit. They promised we wouldn't be bothered again," my father said.

He seemed to believe them, at least for the moment, because he smiled and was quite calm. We talked a little while longer before returning to bed. I couldn't sleep. I had never been so scared in my life, or felt quite so helpless. The vision of my sitting helplessly at the top of the stairs or hiding while my parents were being dragged away was more than I could bear. It reminded me of my father's arrest some months earlier.

I decided there and then that we had to get away, that we could not let ourselves become sitting ducks. We had to find a place to hide or try to escape to Switzerland. A friend of Nora's, Joop, was deeply involved in the Dutch resistance and was the leader of underground groups smuggling people across the border. We talked with him and learned about the details and the two thousand guilders required. Joop daily put his life and family on the line to save others. His face, framed by long, wavy, gray hair, was deeply lined and compassionate, and inspired trust. He was like an actor in a play who appeared out of nowhere and disappeared in the dark. We asked some non-Jewish business associates of my uncle for financial assistance for our escape, but they were afraid of being implicated if we were caught, and regretfully refused to help.

I frequently spent nights with Hans, a school friend, who was not Jewish. Whenever there were rumors of a roundup he was ready to hide me. He also helped me obtain a false identity card—one without a *J*—with my picture but a false name.

In these circumstances we celebrated Yom Kippur. I went with my father to the synagogue in Amsterdam. Watching the congregation, I felt deeply apprehensive about their helplessness. It seemed as if by praying to God all of us, including my parents and me, sought to forget that we were merely waiting for our extermination. I felt angry and determined to do something at all cost.

I discussed with my parents the urgency of their going into hiding, but to my dismay Father stubbornly refused to onderduiken. He did not want to burden or endanger others. Deeper down he must have felt like giving up, as if the strain were becoming unbearable. My mother seemed even more depressed and less able to act. They reflected a general mood of surrender, as if the end could not come too soon. The one straw they, especially my father, continued to cling to was the rumored opening of a second front. Actually, there had been an attempted landing on the French coast. In August 1942, there was a probe at Dieppe, between Le Havre and Calais. Our first awareness of this raid came via the radio, with the usual German propaganda and distortions: the Allied forces were going nowhere and would be destroyed in very short order. The BBC was also vague about the landing but more encouraging, making it easier for us to discount the German claims. As a matter of fact we all, especially my father, felt very excited. Perhaps this was the beginning of the second front. The Allies were at least tying down German troops needed on the eastern front. The Russians had been clamoring for this kind of relief. In a couple of days we learned that the Allied forces had abandoned their beachhead.* The cavalry was not coming to the rescue, not yet.

*Of the 5,000 men who made it ashore, all but 1,500 were lost (Charles B. MacDonald, *The Mighty Endeavor* [New York: Oxford University Press, 1969]).

VII

In early October 1942 Nora's parents were arrested for listening to Allied radio broadcasts. Nora went to the police station immediately to see what she could learn and was herself detained. She had recently been complaining of stomach pains and had been checked for ulcers. The results had been positive. At the police station she suddenly doubled up with pain and carried on until she was allowed to see a doctor; she promised to return later that evening. She called me at the hospital, and I turned to Anton's parents for help. Through their underground contacts they found a hiding place for Nora with a family in the eastern part of the country, and taking only basic necessities with her, she left immediately for Overijsel. We arranged to keep in touch by mail or phone, if necessary.

I decided to try to escape to Switzerland. Since the Nazis were looking for Nora, they most likely would come after me, too. I got in touch with Joop, our underground contact, and got the needed money together, including English pounds. The plan was that I was to go to the Belgium border via Utrecht, where Nora was to join me at the railway station platform. Joop was to meet us at the border station, signal us with a flashlight, and lead us to whoever was going to take us across to Belgium.

In retrospect it sounds so well thought out and routine. But I don't know if I ever have been faced with a more difficult, momentous, and painful decision. It meant taking leave of my parents, probably forever. I had to draw on some of their by no means plentiful funds. I found myself at the same crossroads as earlier at IJmuiden, the day before Holland had surrendered, when I had been offered the chance of escaping on a fishing boat with room for one more passenger. That time I had chosen to stay with my parents. Now I felt there was no point in staying in Amsterdam with them. They refused to go into hiding. Also, there was Nora. We needed each other. I rationalized that once out of Holland I would be able to explore the best route to Switzerland and help my parents escape. I tried to cheer myself up by imagining myself in Switzerland, free, in the Alps, at medical school in Basel or Geneva. I worried over the risks, which I knew were very great, and joked about taking warm clothes along in case I made a wrong turn and ended up in Poland. There were arguments with my mother about her readiness to let others in the house use the kitchen when it was her turn. I worried lest she let people take advantage of her. I needed so urgently to make a show of protecting my parents before I left.

On the afternoon of 20 October 1942, I left Amsterdam. I embraced my parents, telling them and myself that I would see them soon again. Just as I was about to leave, my father stopped me to give me his blessing. He did so in the traditional Jewish fashion. We both felt choked up but neither of us cried. I left in a daze and never looked back.

VIII

The walk to the station was uneventful. I felt strangely calm, secure with my false identity card. The familiar ride to Utrecht was over in no time. I found Nora exactly where Joop had said she would be. We felt immensely relieved to see each other. It was our first meeting since her detention and escape. I admired her courage and inventiveness. In the dim light of the station she looked more Eurasian than Jewish, with her slightly prominent cheekbones, long black hair, and slender body.

The train we boarded took us to a little village south of Eindhoven on the Belgian border. For safety's sake we decided to travel in different compartments. I felt surprisingly calm, almost euphoric. It was as if I were embarking on an exciting trip that would bring us to freedom and a new life in a beautiful country. Already I felt free of the burden of being persecuted by the Nazis for being a Jew. I was the man on the identity card in my pocket, a person just like the others in the compartment, equal once again. I assumed Nora was in the same high spirits. The conductor checked my ticket. Some people got on, others got off at the various stops. Everything went smoothly. At our destination we met Joop as arranged, and he took us to a house in the center of the town. There we found another, older couple sitting at the kitchen table. There were also two men, one of whom was going to guide the four of us across the border. The older couple spoke with a pronounced German accent. We had to wait for about an hour for the "appointed time," when we were to find a car and driver at the other side to take us on to France.

We left with our guide at the set time and soon were on the road to the border. About half a mile before we reached it we left the road and walked through the fields at about half a mile's distance from and parallel to the road. Our guide told us to walk as quietly as possible.

It was dark and eerie. I heard a dog bark and was frightened that the Nazis would detect us. I felt exposed, trudging through the open fields. My heart was in my throat, and I kept hoping that Joop's organization had bribed the border guards. It did not occur to me that these border guards might easily have betrayed the whole escape setup, but all the same I was indescribably apprehensive. We could have been gunned down at any moment. It was one of the longest half hours I ever lived through, and I was already beginning to dread undergoing another such ordeal when crossing into France. Perhaps the agony I experienced was in part due to my leaving my homeland, my parents and friends, a familiar way of life, to escape the Nazi clutches in search of freedom. Finally we turned left, swinging back toward the road, and our guide, with relief in his voice, announced that we had made it. The car was supposed to be waiting for us, but none was there. The arrangements apparently had run into a snag, but our guide reassured us that there were alternate plans. We continued to walk along the road, which was completely deserted because of the 11:00 P.M. curfew.

We trudged on for about five miles before reaching a little farmhouse. The people living there told us our car was expected in a few hours. In the meantime we were free to wait in another car parked in the backyard. I felt uneasy, but we had little choice. It seemed as if we were under a kind of spell, unable to take our intuitive warning signals seriously. Neither Nora nor the other couple expressed any serious doubts; nor did they suggest that we strike out on our own. Finally, toward 4:00 A.M., the driver and car arrived. We felt encouraged. Nora sat next to the driver, and the other couple and I sat in the back seat. At some point the driver, speaking Dutch-Flemish, told us we would first go to Brussels, and there we would get the papers for France. Nobody said anything or questioned why these had not been prepared in advance. Looking back, I cannot believe that we could have been so gullible. We even offered the man chocolates, which he refused. Did he perhaps think they were poisoned?

After a long ride, we came to the outskirts of Brussels. He stopped at a café; we had some coffee, and he called the office where we presumably were to get our papers. I saw a man peer into the café and wondered what he was looking for at 6:00 A.M. After half an hour we departed and drove into the city and into a garage. Abruptly, in German, a man ordered us to get out, and seeing his uniform I realized that we had been taken to the Gestapo.

Just as powerful as the shock of this sudden calamity was the "spell" I mentioned earlier. I was prepared to believe that this was all part of a scenario to get us our false papers—that of course the Germans had been bribed and were just acting in their usual brutal manner as a coverup. The driver had disappeared the instant we stopped. A Nazi Grüne Polizei led all of us into a glassed-in cubicle, one of about six such areas in a large hall. The glass partitions went up three-fourths of the way to the ceiling.

The first cubicle was occupied by a Nazi guard; a radio blared forth German marches and songs, and a large red swastika flag could be seen through the window. I asked Nora what she thought was happening. With calm certainty she stated that we undoubtedly were Nazi prisoners. I disagreed, clinging to the illusion that this was part of the plan to get us our papers. I wavered between thinking that this was the end—that we were trapped—and that it was all part of a prepared script. After about two hours of this vacillation the uncertainty was becoming unbearable.

I walked up to the guard, who told me to sit down and wait. I don't remember exactly how long it took, probably several hours, before I decided that we had been betrayed. This was the end of our road to freedom. There was nothing more I could do but accept whatever *they* were going to do with us. It was all over. Somehow this put an end to my intolerable doubts. I relaxed and told Nora that I felt better because I had given up all hope.

After about four hours we were each in turn taken upstairs for questioning. I was led into an office with a few chairs and a desk, behind which a fat, bald German Grüne Polizei officer was seated.

My earlier doubts returned, and I asked the man whether he was going to help us. He seemed dumbfounded. He did not answer, and after a short silence asked me to fill out a form. Feigning ignorance, I explained that I was unable to answer a number of the questions, most of them concerning money. Neither did I name any names. Nora and I had agreed beforehand to tell them we were married. I had a vision of Rodin's *Burghers of Calais,* identifying with the agitated young man hiding behind the old man who was resigned in the face of certain death.

I pleaded with the man to let us go. I told him that I was still young, a physician with most of my life before me, at the beginning of my career, and asked how he could condemn me to death.

He just continued to sit stolidly behind his desk, told me that there was nothing he could do for me, and ordered me to keep quiet. Then he called Nora in. She did not reveal anything new. He took our false identity cards, looked through the clothing in my case, and sent us downstairs again with our belongings. After another couple of hours we were led to a car with two sinister-looking men in the front seat wearing the kind of hats and raincoats seen in gangster movies. We were crowded in with the other couple who had been stopped with us, and after a short ride through Brussels we arrived at a prison called St. Gilles, after a nearby church of that name.

The driver honked his horn, and the heavy wood-and-steel gate opened. More sinister-looking men were standing around. We were taken to a registry where we were relieved of our valuables, like my watch, and then were led through a long hall to a steel gate. At this point Nora was taken away. We had no time to say good-bye. When I saw the gate close behind her, my passivity evaporated. I shook with rage. I swore I was going to get even with those savages, come what might.

IX

Passing through several gates, I was taken upstairs and put into a cell with two other young fellows. An unpleasant musty odor permeated the room, probably from the chemical toilet in the corner. There was a small, barred window high up and a small table and chair. I was given a blanket and a soup bowl and told about the rules, which were posted on the wall, as in a hotel room. The only thing missing was the rate schedule. During the day we were not allowed to lie down on the cot or on the floor, or to scream—only to breathe. When the door opened we had to stand at attention in the rear of the cell.

One of my cellmates, Piet, a boy of perhaps fifteen, the son of a Flemish farmer, had no idea why he had been arrested—perhaps because his name was on a list of soccer players captioned "Vive le Roy," or perhaps because some acts of sabotage, like cutting telephone lines, had been committed in his area. He had been picked up with about twenty others. He seemed rather resigned and had little if any idea of what was happening in the world. My other cellmate, Pierre, was a thin, tall, hollow-cheeked man in his early twenties, with large, somewhat protruding dark eyes. A member of the resistance, he had killed one of his persecutors after a lengthy chase. He showed me the hole in his pants just over his pocket through which he had fired his gun. He had been interrogated repeatedly but had remained unresponsive. He had planned to become a teacher and perhaps go to the Belgian Congo.

By the time our first meal arrived at noon we felt as if we had known each other for a long time. I had no appetite and gave Piet my soup. (Only days later I could not imagine how I could have been so generous. By then I was starved and would have eaten anything.) In the late afternoon we got some ersatz coffee and a small piece of bread. As soon as the lights were turned off I settled down on the floor on a blanket. The floor was hard, but I was so exhausted it did not bother me very much. Somehow I took pride in being in prison, having stood up against the oppressors. I identified with my cellmate Pierre, who had killed a Nazi, and in some inexplicable way felt more relaxed because I had actively resisted my enemies.

I was grateful that my father had encouraged us in our love of sailing and camping, and thus acclimated us to rugged outdoor life. I also thought of Nora. Where could they have taken her? With whom was she sharing a cell? Would we be able to get in touch with each other? My roommates told me about a camp near Mechelen, not far from Brussels, where Jewish families were allowed to live together. They did not know anything about deportations to Poland.

I slept remarkably well until the morning, when someone banged on the door. This meant that we had to wash at the little basin in the corner and get dressed for inspection and breakfast: coffee and a small piece of bread. That over with, there was not much to do except read. Pierre had some books and old newspapers that he had received with some food packages from his mother.

When everything seemed quiet we heard knocking on the heating pipes, and soon a "phone" conversation about the war was under way between Pierre and the people in the adjoining cell. The source of news usually was a prisoner who worked in the kitchen or offices and had access to a radio. Another channel of communication was the window. We would stand on a chair to look out and listen to what the others above, next to, or below us had to report. These exchanges usually took place in the late afternoon, when the guards were changing and did not pay much attention to us. Another method was to write a message on a piece of paper, tie it to a string with a heavy object, and either lower it to the cell below or swing it to the right or the left. Somebody would stand watch to listen for the footsteps of approaching guards on the metal grating.

This precarious way of maintaining contact with fellow prisoners and Nazi victims symbolized our fight against the excruciating agony of isolation and our need to preserve a sense of belonging to human society, a world where life had meaning and hope. Slowly but persistently, this very elementary connectedness with other human beings had been eroding even before the actual invasion of my country. Friends and members of my family had moved away from Holland. Travel was ever more limited; even phone conversations became unsafe. I realized I had begun to depend for such a source of replenishment on an ever-narrowing group of people, with which Nora was the last remaining link. Now she was out of reach, too. Pierre impressed me as a man I could admire, understand, and eventually trust. He was very determined in his hatred of the Nazis, but there was also something gentle, compassionate, and wise about him that made it easy for us to become friends. We were both living under a death sentence, I for the crime of having been born a Jew and Pierre for having killed someone. I began to sense the crucial importance of such a personal relationship to my will to survive.

By the third or fourth day I began to feel really hungry, which was a new experience. Pierre would sometimes share cake or bread from his food packages with us. These were special treats, and I would eat slowly, savoring every crumb. Once a day, weather permitting, we were marched to a courtyard for half an hour of exercise.

Although conversation was strictly forbidden, these

airings usually gave us a chance to talk to others. They also allowed us a glimpse of the outside world. Although the yard was surrounded by a high brick wall, the neighboring houses towered above it, and sometimes it was possible to see people through the windows. This made me feel both angry and nostalgic, and I dreamed of a hundred and one impossible ways of escape. Pierre mentioned feigning illness or actually becoming sick by smoking a cigarette with aspirin in it to gain admission to the prison infirmary. Escape from the infirmary was presumably possible. Piet once tried the cigarette-cum-aspirin method, but all it did was make him sleepy.

After about a week that seemed more like a month, a fourth man, Gerrit, joined our cell. He was older, in his late fifties. He had come from the south of Holland via the same route as I, and had probably been betrayed by the same people. The owner and manager of a textile mill, he was Jewish, but his wife was not. His "mixed" marriage would supposedly have protected him from deportation, yet he had tried to escape. We talked at length about events in the outside world; things did not sound good at all. Food was getting scarcer, and Jews were being rounded up systematically. In Holland they were sent to Westerbork, in Belgium to Mechelen. When these camps filled up, transports to the east, mostly to Poland, were organized to take care of the overflow.

At first I was allowed to write one letter per week, which I sent to a friend in Amsterdam. I knew that it would be censored, so I wrote only in generalities while still trying to give some idea of what was happening; I also mentioned that it was possible to send food. With the money I had on deposit in the "admissions office" I bought an unlined copybook and pencils from the prison commissary. Pierre had a ruler, and to pass the time I began to make elaborate sketches of the house Nora, our children, and I would live in when the war was won and we were free again. I had a great deal of time to devote to this fanciful daydream and made detailed plans of every floor and room. My dreams were an expression of a profound sense of hope and optimism in the face of insuperable odds. I don't believe I could have survived without them. When I sketched my dream house I could see myself outside the prison walls, feel free, and be with the people I loved. Even though they were a fantasy, these moments were very precious.

One afternoon I was taken out for a physical checkup and joined a line of other prisoners at the infirmary. As we edged forward I was startled to see a file of women. I looked for Nora but did not see her. I had previously asked the guard whether I, being a doctor, could work in the hospital but had received no response. I repeated my inquiry now. In reply, the doctor informed me that since I would not be staying very much longer it was not feasible to grant my request. But my disappointment evaporated when, walking slowly by the row of women, I spotted Nora. We managed to hold hands and talk briefly. She told me we were scheduled to go to Mechelen.

It is difficult to describe how much this brief encounter meant to me. Suddenly I was no longer alone.

The next day Pierre was to stand trial. Convinced that his case was hopeless, he was planning to tell off the "judges" and be as uncooperative as possible. When he returned he told us he had done exactly what he had set out to do; he had told them to go to hell. Nothing was said about his sentence, at least as far as we knew. But several days later, in the evening, he was taken out of our cell. We knew instinctively we would never see him again. Still, our goodbyes were as casual as though he were leaving for only a day. He did not return. The next day the guard came to collect his belongings. We divided the food he had saved. Sad and frightened, I found it difficult to accept that Pierre had been murdered. Obviously the denial of death is not only the privilege of children. When you are as helpless as a child it is the only way out.

A couple of days later Piet was released. They must

have decided that he was harmless. The next day another young man, Jan, joined us. Ours was a busy hotel. Jan seemed rather stupid, but perhaps this was only an act. He claimed that he came from Holland near Amsterdam, was not Jewish, and had been wandering around when one day he was picked up by the regular police for vagrancy.

About a week later Jan was told he was going to be released in a couple of days, and Gerrit and I gave him some letters written on scraps of paper. Mine was to be sent, or better still handed, to a non-Jewish friend who could send it on to my parents. I did not trust Jan enough to give him my parents' address.

Having now become the senior occupant of our cell, I took charge of the communications via the heating pipe and window, and occasionally via the prisoner who brought us our food. I tried to get some word to Nora in this way.

Finally, after a month in prison, on the evening of 19 November 1942, my father's birthday, I was told I'd be going to Mechelen. I packed my sketchbook and pencils and spent a sleepless night worrying about what would happen. The next day after breakfast the guard came and took me downstairs to the admissions office. Nora was there along with several others, including the couple with whom we had left Holland. I talked with Nora about escaping. We seriously discussed the possibility of jumping out of a truck and meeting at a prearranged rendezvous in Brussels.

When they took us outside we were ordered into a canvas-covered truck and told that anyone who attempted to escape would be shot summarily. To underscore that this was no idle threat, two guards with automatics were posted at the rear of the truck at the only possible exit. If all of us had jumped the guards some might perhaps have made it, but nobody seemed ready to organize such a feat. Now and then I got a glimpse of the outside world, and a short while later we drove through a heavily guarded gate into a big square courtyard surrounded by two-storied white stone barracks. We had entered a new world.

X

We were processed again and had to surrender all money and valuables, including watches. Nora and I had decided to "register" as husband and wife. Later this became very important. Our new "home" was an area about six feet square, consisting of two side-by-side straw mattresses in the middle of a large platform along the long wall of a rectangular dormitory, one flight up in a building on the south side of the quadrant, close to its eastern corner. Opposite us was the same kind of platform with a second one above it. Altogether in this dormitory there were about fifty people—men, women, and some children—all Jewish. The Belgians were housed in two dormitories on the opposite side of the quadrant. They enjoyed preferential status and were at least temporarily protected against transportation to the east. They had seniority in the camp, and most of them received regular food packages. This made them part of an elite. When I visited them I felt that they had installed themselves in the dormitory as if it would be home for the rest of the war, amidst an amazing quantity of possessions. I noticed bedsheets in addition to the blankets we were given, and even pots and pans.

When Nora was searched on arrival she had been smarter or more courageous than I. She had managed to hide a knife, a pair of scissors, and a diary. I noticed that most people who had been in the camp for more than a month were very thin and walked with a sort of shuffle, their knees somewhat bent, as if not sure they could keep themselves upright. I learned the reason for this at our first meal. It consisted of a few tablespoons of watery soup with some fibrous pieces of root vegetables, an occasional piece of potato, and virtually no protein or fat.

The fact that Nora and I were reunited helped us to cope with much of the misery we were to face. We were soon introduced to the concentration camp tactics of the S.S. in charge. There was an *Obersturmführer*, a man with a ruddy complexion, dark hair and eyebrows, and four stars on a black square on his collar designating his rank. He rarely walked through the camp but stayed in his quarters, which looked out on the square. His subordinates, especially a tall, thin, rather dark-skinned young sergeant, would make everybody perform strenuous exercises like push-ups, running, lying down and getting up again in rapid succession, and standing at attention for hours, especially in rain or snow or mud. The S.S. overlord would look out of the window and watch the whole incredible scene with a sadistic smile. He obviously loved to see people squirm. Much of the time he was drunk.

The first night was a relief in many ways. Nora and I felt very close to each other. We seemed to be secure at least for the night; a strange sense of safety pervaded us. We were warm under our two blankets. To the right and left of us, barely a foot away, were strangers. Yet we had a peculiar sense of privacy, as if the others were not really there. Before the lights were turned off, the prisoner in charge of running the camp, a German Jew appointed by the S.S., had come to our dormitory and explained the rules, trying to be as reassuring as possible, presenting himself as fatherly, and wished us all a good night.

In the course of the next few weeks my education in the life in a prison camp progressed, my basic drive for survival my only weapon. Carl, a friendly, dark-haired, athletic-looking fellow prisoner of Polish-German descent, seemed to know his way around. During a workout period in the courtyard, I was struck by his obvious effort to perform the exercises with the utmost vigor and precision, as though he wanted to make a good impression on Sergeant Willy, the S.S. torturer and sadist. Carl would be the first to stand at attention, his body straight, his hands at the seams of his pants, clicking his heels. I could not understand what he was putting himself out for and felt revolted by his fawning on the S.S. Once I almost got into a fight with him. If it hadn't been for Nora's calming influence, who knows what would have happened? Carl had been in a concentration camp in Germany and knew how to get himself into those levels of the camp society where the power and the food were. It was difficult for me to adjust to these new values.

If I had thought I knew what hunger was, I soon found I had been greatly mistaken. The food we were given was totally inadequate, especially in winter. The lucky ones received weekly or even semiweekly food packages or, if they were staff, got better food rations. Nora and I learned to ask some people whom we got to know, including some on the staff, to give us their leftover soup rather than throw it away, and at mealtimes we waited until the soup dispenser got to the bottom of the big kettle, where the soup was less watery. Nora seemed to take hunger better than I. After a month my weight was down to 100 pounds, if that, from my normal 140. The camp population could be divided into two groups—those with thin, hollow faces and protruding ribs and shoulder blades and those with a solid layer of fat and muscle; there were very few in between. Food was like money, power, respect, and influence. I realized that in this sort of camp our customary system of values had almost ceased to exist, and with it the possibility of uniting the prison population against the oppressor. In the camp, people were useless. The only purpose of their existence was to serve the oppressor's sadistic needs. The

S.S. was fascinated by and even encouraged internal conflict or self-destructive, competitive behavior. They loved to delegate limited power to a select few, for whom it became a vehicle of survival. In fact, the actual running of the concentration camp was in the hands of prisoners who were selected and supervised by the S.S.

I concluded that in essence it was every man for himself, with a few crucial exceptions. I do believe that a certain degree of primary aggression is inherent in the human race. Freud discussed this in his correspondence with Einstein about war. Yet the reverse is also true; no matter what the circumstances, such human attributes as compassion and altruism cannot be completely eradicated. Some close, very important relationships were formed and maintained in concentration camps, but only in small groups. This became apparent to me only later in Auschwitz, not in Mechelen.

There was a camp doctor, a Jew from Germany, with previous camp-life experience. His realm was in the corner next to the entrance gate adjacent to an administrative office, also run by a Jew from Germany. The doctor had a lay assistant, and I soon realized that the two did not tolerate any intrusion into their zealously guarded domain. I had innocently offered my services, which he had accepted gracefully, but even though I showed up regularly there was nothing for me to do. His helper told me I could come to get some of their leftover special porridge, a farinaceous soup far more nourishing than the standard fare. However, even this treat disappeared after a short while, and it became increasingly difficult to find any extra food. I began to experience the same weakness in the knees that I had seen in others when I first arrived.

I think it was in January 1943, a cold and damp month, that I happened to talk with a man from Belgium, the only non-Jewish inmate. His crime was homosexuality. He liked to dress as a woman. He told me he did not need his soup because he received food packages, and that if I came to his dormitory right after mealtime he would give me the soup. I did so twice. The third time, he happened not to be in, and I asked his roommates if they knew where I could find him. Perhaps they thought I was a homosexual too. Before I knew what was happening, I was punched, cursed at, and pushed down the stairs. I felt humiliated, helpless, and enraged. I ran back to Nora in our dorm, unable to hold back my tears. I could not believe that one Jew could treat another so cruelly, especially when he did not have the physical strength to defend himself.

Both Nora and I had reached what seemed the nadir of our existence. Each mealtime we felt and acted like beggars, having to find food somewhere just to stay alive. Occasionally we were given a salted, dried fish that looked like herring, which provided us at least with some protein. In better days I would have found the idea of eating every scrap, including the head, utterly disgusting, but now I no longer cared as long as it had some nutritive value. I even scraped the bottom of the empty soup kettles for the few pieces of roots left in them.

At that point we belonged to almost the lowest social stratum of camp society. If it had not been for Nora, who as a flutist helped to organize some musical activities, and if we had not become friendly with another Dutch couple, the former owners of a shoe factory, we would not have survived much longer. We even got some space assigned as a workroom and helped stitch slippers from patterns made by the Dutch couple. This allowed us to stay inside when there were roll calls or exhausting exercises.

Gradually, as the camp began to fill up, more people from Holland arrived, among them a physician about twenty years my senior, his wife, and their three young children, who had followed Nora's and my footsteps and had also been betrayed. When Jan, my cellmate in St. Gilles, had been released, I had given him a message for

Joop telling him that the escape organization had been infiltrated. Apparently new channels had been formed, but they too had been infiltrated.

My newly arrived colleague and I could talk about the good old days, of our medical work and careers, of our future dreams. I knew a cousin of his in Bloemendaal very well. His dormitory also housed a young man, about eighteen years old, who was a gifted guitarist and had managed to hold onto his instrument. He loved Bach, and we would listen to him play with an intensity I had seldom experienced before. Ever since, Bach has held a special meaning for me. The contrast between the purity of his music and our misery seemed to imbue every phrase with special depth. The horror of our situation made the beauty of life so much more poignant and precious.

By January the camp was filled to the rafters, and rumors about an imminent transport flew about. Usually the subject of going east was not discussed. The defeats suffered by the German Army in Russia were a far more popular topic. We knew of them from reports of prisoners who cleaned the S.S. quarters or from newspapers used as wrapping for food packages or otherwise smuggled into the camp. Some prisoner-trustees were allowed to go into town like regular employees. The chief advantage of such staff positions was immunity from transport. Despite the misery here, the thought of leaving this camp was nevertheless frightening. We had very few illusions about our chances of survival in Poland. Some claimed they might be greater, that we would have to work but would be better fed. I, for one, put no stock in these stories. I felt a deep sense of doom, a kind of black despair, and so I tried not to think or talk about it.

And then one day it actually happened. A transport was scheduled to leave the camp in a week. Nora and I prepared ourselves as best we could. I was told they would make me the transport physician, which would enhance my chances in the new camp. We had resigned ourselves to our fate when, altogether unexpectedly, I was informed that I would not join the transport but would stay on in Mechelen as the assistant camp doctor. I asked that Nora also be allowed to stay, to work as a nurse. The request was granted. We could hardly believe our luck. It was like a reprieve from a death sentence.

The next day Henk, the older physician, approached me and suggested anxiously that given his experience he was far better qualified for the job than I, and moreover he had a wife and three children. He also said that being much older than I he didn't stand a chance of survival, that Nora and I were young and strong and could make it. I told him that age did not make much difference but that I was willing to let the commandant decide which of us should stay. That morning we both appeared before the commandant, an S.S. *Untersturmführer.* He asked whether I was voluntarily ceding my place to Henk. I said that I could not possibly make that decision but would abide by his. He answered that he would let us know that afternoon.

After what seemed endless hours of suspense and agony, Nora and I were called to the camp doctor's office. Again we had to wait; the doctor and the commandant went outside to talk things over. Nora and I waited without saying a word. I had already resigned myself to being shipped out when the doctor came back and informed us that we would stay. I felt strange about my good fortune. We decided to keep it very quiet. Henk, desperate, was furious with me, as if I were the one responsible. I could and would not do anything more about it. I assumed that the camp doctor did not want an experienced physician as his assistant. Perhaps he feared that a more seasoned doctor might prove to be superior to him and replace him, in which case he himself might be transferred. Apparently I posed the lesser threat.

On the day of the transport, between eight hundred and a thousand people were lined up in the courtyard, divided into groups, and led to cattle cars on a railroad siding outside the camp. The exodus started around noon, and by late afternoon everybody except the staff, Nora, and I had left. It was eerie. People we had befriended were gone. There was nobody to talk to, no voices and sounds, only emptiness and silence.

I thought that even if we were scheduled for the next transport the weather would then be warmer and our chances better. Also, miraculously, we had received a package some days earlier. From its contents—food, warm socks, and gloves—I knew it must have come from my parents in response to a letter I had sent from St. Gilles or maybe one passed on by Jan, my former cellmate. It seemed as if we had indeed weathered our deepest level of deprivation and were on the way up. The extra food our new position gained us, even though relatively meager, was precious. We savored every morsel, eating very slowly to make it last forever. There was also the hope for another parcel. But, most important of all, it was a contact with the world we had left.

With the camp nearly empty we moved to a different dormitory, a somewhat warmer room one floor below the Belgian floor. It suddenly seemed as though we had become part of the "staff," since they were the only ones left. There were no drills, and in general the S.S. paid little attention to us. I wondered, as did others, whether this was related to Germany's frontline defeats. I began to feel more optimistic; perhaps there was a chance we would survive. Rumors even began to circulate that the transports would cease. I borrowed a copy of Voltaire's *Candide* from a newly arrived fellow prisoner and enjoyed it almost as much as our food package, savoring every word.

The workshop where we made slippers had closed since the people with the expertise had gone. Some of us formed a little orchestra and a band; the staff managed to get music and instruments. Nora played the flute. There was a cello but no scores, and because I was poor at memorization and improvisation I did not join in. Somebody used the cello in the jazz band, plucking the strings. Not only did the soup rations seem improved, but the bread ration got bigger. I began to gain weight, and the weakness in my knees disappeared. But the camp was filling up again. Every week new prisoners arrived.

Head lice were discovered in one of the dormitories. Various remedies were tried, including kerosene rinses, but they were of no help. The S.S. decided that those who were infested, and anybody else who volunteered, could go to the quarantine facilities in the Antwerp harbor for delousing. This seemed to offer an unusual possibility of escape, so we decided to go. We were to ride on a streetcar that ran from just outside our camp in Mechelen to the Antwerp harbor. Nora and I discussed escape plans and rendezvous. We even wondered if we should return to Holland and hide or try to move on toward Switzerland. We had learned from several people, including an entire family that had been taken prisoner and brought to Mechelen, that they had actually crossed into Switzerland, only to be arrested for illegal entry and shipped back to France. We decided nonetheless that we would try our luck.

The actual trip to Antwerp was very strange. We traveled on a regular streetcar reserved for us. It almost seemed like a school outing. The sole reminders of our prisoner status and the war were the two S.S. men on each of the two cars and the sadistic S.S. sergeant in charge of our drills. The only weapons they carried were the guns in their side holsters. It was impossible to jump off the car because that would have involved passing by the S.S. men guarding both the front and rear platforms. When we got to the quarantine facilities the women went one way, the men another. We had to hang up our clothes. They were to be fumigated while we went to the showers, where we could stay under the hot water and wash with "green" soap for close to a half hour, an unexpected, unbelievable luxury. The S.S. men came by frequently to make sure we were all still there, but without clothes we had little choice. Even so, when we were dressing we heard that one person was missing. We had to stand at attention for a long time while they searched the premises. They looked in the spaces between the ceiling and roof of the shower compartments, but nobody was found. The S.S. were furious and threatened to make us pay. Finally we returned to the streetcar, where Nora rejoined me. Neither of us had managed to escape. Furious and upset, she told me how the S.S. had spent a long time watching the women shower and that one had taken her gold engagement ring and accused her of planning to use it to buy her escape. She complained to the commandant, and to our amazement she got the ring back the next day.

When we returned to the camp we had to stand at attention for several hours as a punishment for the escape of one of our group. Also, it appeared that escape from the camp itself was possible. A few days after our return a young man from Holland managed to get away over the roof and into the garden of the adjacent convent, where he was found the next day hiding in a closet. He was brutally beaten, his head was shaved, and he was put into solitary confinement for several weeks.

Yet on the whole life in the camp was becoming more tolerable. We received food packages almost weekly, the weather was getting warmer, and we managed to sit in the sun for brief spells. The war news was also becoming more favorable. The Nazis were being stopped or beaten back on all fronts. There appeared to be an obvious correlation between the greater tolerance of the S.S., the improvement in the food, and the Allied victories.

At the end of March 1943, it seemed that as the food improved, romances and sexual affairs among the staff became more commonplace. Perhaps it was the spring weather. For almost ten months I had experienced little sexual desire, and Nora had not either. Others reported similar reactions, and we wondered whether this was due to some additive to our soup or simply because of the generally deficient diet.

Meanwhile the deadly business of filling up the camp in preparation for the next transport, about which there was talk again, continued without letup. A Belgian Jew who knew a person whose address in Brussels I had been given by my father prior to leaving Holland told me that he had top-secret information that the next transport would be attacked and stopped by partisans before it could reach the Belgian-German border. I also began to wonder and worry about whether Nora and I would again be spared and allowed to stay at Mechelen. At first I was told that we would, but then the doctor became evasive. I took this as a bad omen. There was also talk that this transport was going to a camp in Germany, or perhaps to Theresienstadt in Czechoslovakia, not to Poland.

Finally, 18 April 1943 was set as the day of the transport. All of us, including Nora and me, were given numbers to wear. This made it definite; we, too, were going. We pleaded, but to no avail. Another doctor and I were appointed as transport doctors, and we were told that this would improve our chances regardless of our destination. I did not believe it.

On the crucial day, after the usual standing around and waiting, we were herded into cattle cars with wooden bars nailed to the outside of the small windows to make them escape-proof. Nora and I were the last to be put on the train, in a car with about twenty sick women and several infants lying on the straw-covered floor. A pot served as toilet. One of the women was motionless, moaning, barely alive. Others were propped up along the sides of the car. Nora and I tried to make them as comfortable as possible. There was nothing I could do in my role as doctor. I did have some medical books and a stethoscope, but no medicines. I did not know how I could possibly give medical care, nor did I know what was going on in the other cars.

In the early evening the doors of the train were bolted, and the transport got under way. Light from the setting sun filtered through the small window. We had quite a supply of good food, even some chocolate and milk, which we were given on leaving. As the train began to gather speed, it grew dark, and we ate some of the food. Most of the others, the patients, did not feel like eating.

Nora and I held each other close. We felt terribly alone. The others hardly seemed like human beings any more. We were surrounded by nameless death. We did not know our companions, had never seen them before. The best we could do was to save our strength and sleep as much as we could.

Preoccupied with the possibility of escape, I found sleep difficult. Perhaps the wooden bars across the window could be yanked off. But S.S. guards were all around us, on the roof of the trains, in the front and middle and at the end. Was it possible to climb out without being seen? It would have to be very dark. What if I got out and Nora did not? In my mind's eye I could see myself jumping out a train window, rolling on the ground as though reborn a free man.

XI

The train stopped abruptly, and I woke with a start. Light flashed through the window, and I heard shooting.

"This must be the attack by the partisans I was told about in Mechelen," I said to Nora.

I looked out the window and saw people running through a wooded area, some of them screaming in pain. I tried to knock one of the wooden bars off the window, but to no avail. I just didn't have enough strength. The train began to move again. It seemed as if we had been under way for hours. Surely we must have crossed the Belgian border into Germany. But later we decided that the attack had taken place in Belgium.*

With the approach of dawn we stopped at a German station. The door of our car was opened, and unbelievable though it may seem, I was allowed to walk along the train to see if anyone needed a doctor. My colleague, Albert, who

*This attack was described in detail by Jacob Gutfriend ("The Jewish Resistance Movement in Belgium," in *They Fought Back*, ed. and trans. Yuri Suhl [New York: Schocken Books, 1975]). "The partisans stopped the train by swinging a red light in the middle of the track. They opened the doors of some of the cars, and 600 people were let out of the train. About half were recaptured, 20 killed, and 10 wounded. Eight of the wounded were taken by the Germans to a hospital in Tirlemont, near the attack site. These were later rescued from the hospital by the underground in another daring raid. However, a few of them were rounded up later by the Gestapo with the help of an informer."

with his wife, Sonya, was in another car, had also been let out. There were eighty to a hundred people crammed into each car. We went to one car where we found a man tied up with thin rope, motionless and apparently dead. And all we could do was to hand out aspirins!

I returned to my car, and the train began to move again. To our surprise, the door was left open. It was a sunny spring morning, and the scenery was beautiful. The grass was green, flowers and fruit trees were in bloom—an idyllic scene. But I had only to turn around and see people dying to return to reality. Even so, at various times during this macabre journey I felt a strange sense of curiosity. I was going to a place nobody knew anything about, like an explorer starting out for unknown territory, and I might be the only one to tell the world about it. My fear abated. The dangers ahead seemed less insurmountable. Perhaps life was possible wherever we were going.

The idea of escape was still on my mind, but the train was moving rapidly, it was bright daylight, and I would have made a ready target for the S.S. And even if I managed to get away, where would I go in Germany? Who would help? We were on our way to a far-off place, out of touch with the rest of the world, somewhat like the astronauts who lost contact with earth while on the other side of the moon. This strange isolation from anything or anybody known to us began to set in with relentless force. My whole existence up to that point floated away from me, leaving a gap that could not be closed. It left me focused mostly on the present, the immediate future, and Nora. This state lasted in essence through my whole camp experience. It colored all my relationships, with a few important exceptions.

We kept going all day, making stops at various stations across Germany. When it grew dark the door of our car was bolted again. One of our stops was Berlin, where I saw steam engines with swastikas and slogans about winning the war, and I realized that Theresienstadt was an unlikely destination. We stopped frequently during the night, and I slept little, catching glimpses of what looked like camps with high barbed-wire fences and lights all around, and of coal mines.

After a long stop toward dawn the doors were pushed open, and we were told to hurry out onto a sort of platform. There was a high-ranking S.S. medical officer near us, and I told him in my best German that Nora and I were the nurse and doctor in charge of the transport. He seemed friendly and told us where to stand and not to let anybody move us except on his order, treating us as colleagues. He also told me to hold onto the books I had in my hand, to contact him later at the camp, and that we would be well taken care of. Later I learned that the S.S. medical officer who seemed so polite and collegial was Edward Wirths, the chief doctor of all the camps in the Auschwitz area.

Prisoners from the camp were rushing about taking the sick people off the train to trucks. When I asked one of them where we were, he shushed me, gesturing silence. At one point an S.S. sergeant approached us and told us to move. I told him loudly and clearly that the Obersturmführer had ordered us to stay put, and stay we did. We saw some people being loaded into trucks, and others—mothers and children—walking away and running in rows to a nearby camp, or so I thought. Then Nora and Sonya were told to get into a truck, and a little later Albert and I climbed into another, with about forty men, all rather young. Suddenly Nora was gone. In contrast to my reaction in St. Gilles I was either too bewildered or too numb to feel anguish about being separated from her. Somewhere in the back of my mind I tried to believe the S.S. doctor's promise to take good care of us.

It was daylight when we drove off, and after half an hour's ride we arrived at our destination. I learned later that we were in Germany and that the name of the camp was Buna, near Monowitz. It was surrounded by barbed wire on ten-foot-high cement poles. Some of the barbed wire was attached to insulators and obviously electrically charged. At regular intervals spotlights were mounted on the poles. Also, the camp was ringed by guard towers. Both sides of the main road were lined with row after row of long wooden barracks. Neither the main nor the side roads were paved. We drove to a barracks opposite the entrance, obviously the admission or screening station, where we were ordered to undress. Our clothes were taken from us and our heads were shaved. This, oddly enough, reminded me of freshman hazing at the university. No questions were answered, even though all these tasks were performed by prisoners. When we entered the camp I had looked to see whether the prisoners appeared well fed, and most seemed thin and haggard in their dirty striped uniforms. But those cutting hair and in charge of the showers wore clean uniforms and looked much better in general. I realized they must by veterans, part of the upper strata of camp society.

We were allowed to keep only our shoes. I was wearing a pair of sturdy walking boots. They were not to be mine for very long.

Our shaved heads seemed to me the first obvious physical change that marked us as different from the population outside the camp and contributed to making escape impossible. We were helpless. All we could do was to try to survive in this strange and macabre world, whatever it was going to be, out of touch with the other, familiar world. As yet I had no notion of any of the extermination methods. We took our showers, at least I did, totally unaware that they might be used as outlets for gas. That awareness only came later. We were handed relatively clean caps, striped uniforms, shirts, and underpants.

We walked to what was to be our block or barracks. Two rows of three tiers of bunks were divided by a corridor running down the middle for over half the block. In the center were the entrance and bathrooms with toilets along the side and a trough with faucets in the middle. Everything looked rather new. The floor was spotless and the blankets lay neatly folded, with military precision, on straw-filled pallets. The place smelled of soap, freshly scrubbed. After each of us was assigned a bunk—I got an upper berth by volunteering to haul food from the kitchen—we were called out again. Behind a table sat a prisoner with an implement, who proceeded to tattoo a number and a triangle on our left forearms. He did it with amazing speed, and the number came out rather crooked, not the neat sort of job I was to see later on. Not only was a bodily change being imposed on me, but an irrevocable, irreversible one. It dawned on me that this camp was far more dangerous than either Mechelen or St. Gilles and that I was probably not meant to come out alive. Still, I did not give up hope.

The tattooed number was literally the first irreversible change of my body, imposed on it, like the branding of cattle, at the point of a gun. The number was at that moment and forever after in the realm of the S.S. our only identity. Later I learned that as one survived longer one's personal identity would gradually regain some of its significance. At least in certain situations one's name became important again. After a year my number was treated with a certain awe, even admiration. It indicated that I was becoming an "old timer," one who has experience—an ungodly mark of distinction.

Strangely enough, we were given paper and envelopes and told to write home. I was afraid to write to my parents lest I cause them trouble, so I wrote to Anton's sister and brother-in-law, who were not Jewish, knowing that they would get in touch with my parents if they could. I wrote only in very general terms that I was all right and hoped they were, too. Anything more would have been censored. I was too dazed to worry that the Nazis might use any sign of life to substantiate their claim that Buna and places like it were merely work camps.

By this time it was noon. Our lunch was a bowl of soup of the usual watery consistency. The prisoner in charge, our block's *Kapo*, seemed well fed. A black triangle preceded the number on his prison uniform. We had to write our numbers on a strip of material next to two triangles, one yellow and one red, superimposed to form a Star of David, and sew it to the left front of our jackets. My number was 117641, my only identification. In this sense we ceased to be individuals. The very moment I entered the camp this feeling of being nothing was pervasive, and I was constantly reminded of it by the selfish, impersonal atmosphere. If I thought I knew some of my fellow inmates before we went through what seemed a metamorphosis, now they were strangers. Their faces had taken on a masklike uniformity. The only exception, and thank God there always were exceptions, was Albert, my transport colleague, whose wife had left our lineup together with Nora. His face was still recognizable. He also had volunteered for the kitchen detail, and his bunk was near mine.

After we attended to these details we were called outside to line up. A prisoner meeting an S.S. man or Kapo had to take off his hat, a beretlike affair made of the same striped material as the uniform. In rushing out to the lineup I had left my hat on my bunk. I believe I was the only one without a hat. The Kapo screamed at me to go and get it. When I returned he slapped my face so hard that I fell down. I was too dazed to feel any pain, but I never again forgot my hat. First he made us practice "Hat on, hat off" at least twenty-five times. Then he divided us into small groups. My group's job was to help prisoners, old-timers, to move heavy cement poles like those in the fence around the camp. Four men per pole. It was hard going; the old-timers told us to take it easy but to make it look as if we were busy. The pole moving seemed to have no purpose other than to keep us busy. It was hot, and we stripped off our jackets and undershirts. Thanks to the extra food in Mechelen I was in relatively good shape. This seemed to impress the prisoners in the nearby kitchen. The strong were admired, the weak disdained. They called me into the kitchen and gave me half a loaf of bread. Then it became clear what they were after. One of them wanted my shoes. When I refused, he offered me a pair of riding boots and told me to try them for a while. He also made it clear that if I did not accept the offer he could make life very difficult for me, but that if I did I could always come to the kitchen for bread. The kitchen workers obviously were among the most powerful persons in the camp. I had no choice. I also noticed that he had a red triangle in front of his number, which meant he was a political prisoner, not a Jew. He spoke Polish and broken German.

After the deal was completed I went back to my work group. The brief rest had been welcome, and I realized that if I did not find a way to husband my strength I would not last long. The prisoners who had been in the camp for some time let me in on some of the ways they would protect themselves against the tricks of the S.S. guards. For instance, the S.S. would ask a prisoner to retrieve some object, his own hat or some such thing, from an area near the fence or from some out-of-bounds place and then shoot him. Their alertness to "potential escapes" earned them extra days off.

We returned to our block at about four o'clock. Various work details were assigned, and I became part of the morning coffee detail. This meant I had to get up at 5:00 A.M., about half an hour before the others, but it earned me the privilege of that upper bunk.

The first night I slept soundly until the Kapo woke me in the dark to get the coffee. It was very cold, but carrying the big vat suspended from two poles warmed us up fast. At least we got our coffee and bread first.

At the earliest opportunity I sneaked into the kitchen to see whether I could get my shoes back, because the boots were too large. I was partly successful; I got some reasonably good shoes that fit instead of those clumsy boots. The boots surely would have caused blisters, a possibly very dangerous lesion in this sort of place.

After several days of exhausting work in this camp,

which still seemed in the process of completion, an announcement was read at roll call requesting all physicians, pharmacists, and chemists to report to a man seated at a nearby table. The next morning both Albert and I were told to report to the camp hospital.

While we waited in the hospital, I told Albert that I believed this assignment would save our lives. He did not seem convinced, but I was. Maybe this was what the S.S. physician on our arrival had meant when he told us to get in touch with him. I was put to work as a nurse in one of the barracks of the hospital, a large room with about twenty patients. Most of them were suffering from colds, pneumonia, or boils, and nearly all ran high temperatures. There was another young man, not a physician, who was my helper, and a somewhat older doctor who was our boss. He had a little office at one end of the barracks with a window looking out over fields beyond the fence of the camp. The first day, when I had some time to sit there by myself and look outside, I began to feel more human again, and thought of Nora, where she might be.

In this situation I saw some hope of surviving. The doctor under whom I worked was very helpful; he cared about the patients and seemed to have considerable experience in camp life. We had little to do with the other parts of the camp. We even had our own informal morning and evening roll calls: ten or fifteen people would gather between the blocks of the hospital nonchalantly. There was none of the rigid drill atmosphere of the rest of the camp, in which even the bodies of inmates who had died while working had to be carried to roll call. Our food was also superior. We got at least two bowls of soup and frequently a sort of farina as well. This was also used as a special diet for certain patients. Sometimes during the day we could sneak in a brief nap, an unbelievable luxury. Strange as it may seem, the future was beginning to look a little less bleak.

XII

I began to wonder increasingly where Nora might be and what might have happened to her. I asked a number of people who had spent some time in camps like Buna around Auschwitz. All of them were evasive, but they did mention a camp for women, and one told me that there were also some women in a special block in Auschwitz. Wherever she was, it seemed very far away. I also wondered about my father and mother, hoping and praying that they had gone into hiding. I felt completely isolated from the world I had known. I wondered what the S.S. would do with the letter I had been allowed to write. It did not seem possible that they would allow any message to go through, yet one could always hope—or even, like Candide, believe that all was for the best, or nurse an almost magic faith that one would live to tell the tale.

About three weeks after I began to work in the *Krankenbau*, the hospital, I developed a sore throat that persisted despite energetic gargling; if anything, it got worse. My boss looked at it and suggested I go to the so-called clinic and see a certain older doctor, a German Jewish professor. I did. He thought it was diphtheria and told me to come back the next morning to have the S.S. doctor look at it. I felt I had made a mistake in asking for help. I found out that no prisoners with infectious diseases were allowed in Buna. Now and then I had heard locutions like "going up through the chimney," a reference to the crematorium. Strange how everybody both knew and did not know about the ever-present proximity of death. I had a vague image of Auschwitz as a large complex consisting of many camps, of masses of dehumanized nonpersons working in construction, building roads, performing impossible tasks, dying either from exhaustion or from illness, or being shot by the S.S., all within a short period of time, a couple of months at the most. So far I had been spared that fate, but I worried that my period of grace was about to run out. It was a long day and sleepless night, and the fever only made me feel worse.

The next morning, after the S.S. doctor had seen me, and after waiting in the clinic, I was put in a van with three bodies. I could not hear him clearly, but it seemed that the S.S. doctor said something to the driver about Auschwitz. Off we went. One thought that came to me, perhaps not so strange, was that maybe I would see Nora again. Actually, at that point I was no longer thinking of dying. I could see the countryside, flat farmland, and wondered again about escaping though I knew it was impossible. After half an hour we drove into a camp and stopped in front of one of its big two-story brick barracks. I was let out, taken into a building, undressed, and given a shirt. Somebody took me upstairs to a large ward with many double bunks. I got an upper bunk in the far corner.

I found myself in the company of several other diphtheria victims, two of them also from Holland. A man in the bunk next to me, Kees, was from Amsterdam. He had worked in a bicycle shop in Holland and had come to Auschwitz from Westerbork a month ago. I learned that I was now in the central camp, or *Stammlager*, Auschwitz. Kees obviously enjoyed being able to talk in Dutch about his life in Holland before the war and especially about food, a topic as contagious as an infectious disease. After a week or ten days, as I recovered and my fever subsided, I began to feel famished again. Talking about food and favorite dishes, desserts and cakes, we could imagine eating these delicacies and for a moment forget our hunger. I found out that dreams of lavish meals were common. We would tell each other about the scrumptious dinners we had eaten in our sleep. Of course, hunger kept gnawing away at us. We were not allowed to get out of bed except to go to the toilet. This excursion required the permission of a male "nurse," a fat Russian about my age. Those who stayed too long or had not bothered to ask for permission were chased back to bed with his threats of stepping on their bare toes with his heavy boots. Only food could buy his "favors." Since I was unable to organize any extras, my hunger went unappeased.

I had only the vaguest notion of what was happening in the rest of the ward. My world was confined to a little corner with four or five other sick people and that monster guard. My only contact with the rest of the world was through two corner windows, one looking out on a fifty-foot-wide space between our barracks and the adjoining one, and the other on the camp's "main street," where I had arrived. Daydreaming was my principal activity. Nobody could take this away from me. I imagined all the things I would do when I returned home after the war. I loved to sail. In 1937 our whole family—my parents, brother, sister, and brother-in-law—and some friends had taken a trip on a typical Dutch sailboat called a *boeier*, a spacious barge-like vessel with a tall mast and huge white, billowing sails. So I daydreamed about a beautiful ship made of solid oak, gleaming with varnish that revealed its grain and elaborate carvings, pushing through the blue waters of the Dutch lakes and rivers. I would tell my family and friends tales about the war and its horrors. One day, while looking out toward the main street, I saw a cart in front of the kitchen with two beautiful, prancing horses. I imagined myself at the end of my captivity taking these horses and going home on that cart. Occasionally I would think of writing a play or making a documentary about this "hospital," with its starved, isolated patients and its anti-Semitic, sadistic, well-fed Russian nurse. This sort of wishful thinking made time go by faster.

At irregular intervals an S.S. doctor walked through the ward and talked with the doctor-prisoner in charge of this part of the hospital. On these occasions everybody was quiet, and there was talk of a repeat performance of the recent "selections." This meant that all prisoners had to parade before the S.S. doctor, who would decide whether to send them back to work or to the gas chamber. I somehow managed to forget this bit of information, or at least not to think of it, and fortunately the selection did not materialize.

After I had been in the hospital for about a week a young German joined our "diphtheria corner." Although half-Jewish, he seemed more German than the Germans. I kept my distance, though eventually he mellowed considerably. The fact that he had a red triangle in front of his number and for all practical purposes was not considered Jewish gave him an obvious advantage. His soup came from the bottom of the kettle, with more vegetables and potatoes; he would get extra farina and could move around without incurring the Russian's sadistic wrath. It again became clear to me that Jews, about half the camp's population, were the pariahs of the camp. The rest were Poles, Germans, Czechoslovaks, Russians, and a few West Europeans. With very few exceptions, none of the important jobs were held by a Jew. Most of the Kapos, except those in the hospital, were Germans sentenced for serious crimes like armed robbery or murder. The kitchen workers and other key jobholders were German and Polish non-Jews. As a doctor my position was a little better, but not much. Another member of our little corner was a young Polish Jew, David, rather fresh and smart at getting along with everybody. He was not very ill and was up and about in a week. He was the block elder's special assistant, and there were rumors that he was his homosexual partner. He too received favored treatment. I was particularly struck by his uniform; it looked custom-made, of heavy, flannel-like material. Such an outfit, even a jacket, was an important status symbol, just as in the outside world but more so.

When I began to feel better, after about two weeks, David gave me a little package wrapped in white tissue paper. I opened it, curious and apprehensive. In it was a sardine sandwich on dark bread and a letter from Nora. She was alive!

I am in the same camp as you, only a few hundred feet away in a special block, number 10. Albert was transferred from Buna to here shortly after you. He saw you by chance when you looked out of a window. Sonya is also here. Both of us are nurses taking care of the women who are used for experiments from which Sonya and I as nurses are exempted. Albert helps bring the soup from the kitchen to us, and has talked with Sonya. I hope you feel better. Write me soon. David will get it to me.

Love, hugs and kisses, Nora.

Block 10 was used for "medical research" and "experiments" by the notorious Doctors Schuman and Clauberg. I later learned that they were supposed to find "simple ways" of sterilization by injecting chemicals into the womb to close off the genital pathways. They also used X rays on the ovaries. The subjects of these experiments suffered terribly. My informants stressed the need for secrecy and the danger of talking about what I knew.

This contact with Nora was like a gift from heaven. Had the S.S. doctor at the ramp on our arrival perhaps helped us? I felt incredibly elated. Another real human being was with me, nearby. I was no longer alone. It looked as if the barrier and isolation had been lifted a little. I immediately became something of a celebrity in my little corner of the ward. The chances that husband and wife could get together again in this sort of world were less than one in a hundred thousand. The next day the block elder, Paul, a German political prisoner, came to see me and offered his or his sidekick's services as a mail deliverer. Furthermore, he promised to try to get one of the S.S. women in charge of Nora's block to come over on some "official" business and bring Nora with her and arrange for us to meet in his room or office. It should not be difficult to imagine how this dramatic turn of events made me feel. I could see some possibility of survival, something and somebody to live for. There were people left in this cruel, hellish world who were truly human, who would risk their lives for someone else.

I was able to walk around more and got some clothes, and the Russian left me alone. Paul told me that I could stay in the block and work on a ward once I had recovered completely. Nora and I were now in almost daily contact, exchanging short notes. Paul's helper, Derek, a young Czech, was our mailman. Paul kept his word, and a week after our first contact he told me to expect Nora and an S.S. woman to come over the next morning. I cannot describe my feeling of suspense and anticipation. We had not seen each other for two months, and it felt more like two years. So much had happened.

The next morning, at the appointed time, Derek came to get me, and for the first time I walked through the center of the ward, a strange new world, out the door to a landing at the top of the stairs. At the left a door led into Paul's room and office. I walked in, and there was Nora. She looked amazingly well; she wore a skirt and blouse and was a real human being—the same I had known before Auschwitz. We embraced and held each other very tight for some minutes before I realized that Paul and the S.S. woman were in the room, off in a corner to give us some privacy. Nora and I spoke in Dutch.

I whispered that I couldn't believe we were there to-gether, that it seemed like a miracle to find her looking so well. She said that as a nurse she was supposedly safe from Clauberg's experiments. She lived with fifteen other nurses, Sonya among them, in a separate room on the first floor. I told her of Paul's promise that once I had recovered I could stay and work in the same block I was in now.

Nora kissed me and said that she had even been able to get hold of a flute and had been playing a little. She suggested that once I got well enough to go outside I could volunteer to carry things to her block, such as food. That was how Albert and some others managed to get in.

I asked Nora how on earth she had managed to make the sandwich she had sent me. Smiling, she explained that she had "organized" it with the help of other prisoners, mostly non-Jewish, who got food packages and from time to time distributed tidbits. Food was not a major problem. Two of her roommates were the wives of professors working in a camp laboratory. One even had her little son with her. They were very important, to judge by their preferential treatment. The camp, Nora said, was an extremely strange and dangerous world.

Continuing in Dutch, she lowered her voice and confided to me that this was a death camp, that the type of civilized behavior that had been part of our past had no place here. We were being turned into ciphers or puppets who would submit numbly to torture and death. The block next to hers, Block 11, was the so-called Bunker, an installation that hardly anybody ever left alive. We should consider ourselves fortunate to have met like this, Nora assured me, and she displayed a miraculous conviction that we would get out of this damned hell alive.

At this point Paul indicated that we had better part. Our meeting was not without danger; Derek had been standing watch on the landing. We kissed each other good-bye. I thanked Paul and the S.S. woman, who seemed remarkably friendly, and we each went our way.

Later Paul surprised me by asking why Nora and I had not made love so he could have done the same with the S.S. woman. He was obviously teasing, but I wondered how much sexual involvement there was between prisoners and camp personnel. He must have known this S.S. woman well enough to gain her trust and cooperation. But I did not speculate much further. I was elated.

Paul was a remarkable man. He was tall and wiry, in his early forties, with a finely chiseled face and dark, penetrating eyes. He was a very prominent man in the camp and one of the few among these "prominents" who was not anti-Semitic. The whole business of my meeting with Nora in his room created a bond of friendship with him that gave me strength, yet it also burdened me with a debt I felt I could not repay. But he was not the type of man who thought I was beholden to him. I learned that even in Auschwitz one could find true altruism.

XIII

From that day on, my health improved steadily. My temperature gradually returned to normal, and I was moved downstairs to a smaller room with about twelve bunks. The male nurse there was a wonderful person, a French Jew who had been in various other camps. He was very kind and did everything in his power to help us regain our strength. In the evening he often played a violin that he had somehow managed to lay his hands on. Apparently the S.S. was storing all the belongings of people arriving at the Auschwitz area in huge warehouses, called "Kanada" after the land of plenty. These warehouses, like everything else in and around the camp, were organized and run by prisoners under S.S. supervision. Although taking anything from them was forbidden under penalty of death, it was possible to organize special arrangements, like my meeting with Nora and her getting hold of a flute, despite all the Teutonic discipline and regulations of the S.S. Human concern could not be totally suppressed. It emerged in the most unexpected ways, in defiance of the literal representation of death on the collar and hat of the S.S. uniform.

After six weeks in the sick bay I had completely recovered and was discharged. I was assigned to the tuberculosis ward to work as a nurse with another, experienced nurse and two doctors, one an older Pole, a non-Jew, and one a Czech Jew. The latter was by far the more congenial. I never quite trusted the Polish doctor. He spoke a little French and German, but when it really mattered—during surgical procedures—he always reverted to Polish, which I did not understand, although I began to pick up some simple words and phrases, none related to medicine. The doctors in the camp hospital wore white jackets, not the striped uniform. I was a nurse, so I wore the regular stripes.

Temporarily, at least, I had to sleep in the same ward as the patients. Several double bunks, one above the other, had been set aside in the corner for us. To my dismay I discovered that my bunk, like most of the others, was infested with fleas. After one night I was covered with flea bites. A few days later I found some flea powder; it helped but did not eliminate the problem. One had to be careful not to scratch: the danger of infection was great. Boils and abscesses were widespread, as I observed on my patients. I was also concerned about working on the tuberculosis ward, although most of the cases were supposedly not open T.B., with positive sputum. I tried to be careful and made sure to hold onto my personal utensils, such as bowl and spoon. Most of the patients were in very poor shape. They were thin to the point of emaciation and given to paroxysms of coughing of suffocating intensity. Some hardly touched their food. I tried feeding them, but with limited success. Ben, a young Dutch Jew, was so far gone that he did not even want his little portion of bread. I tried coaxing him to drink some coffee or water, but to no avail. Ben had given up; he did not want to live.

I noticed that other patients, seeing his condition, his abdication of life, had their eyes on his bread and soup. Stealing bread was the worst crime anyone could commit, punished by often fatal beatings. Although in the hospital the debility of the victims precluded such retaliation, both staff and patients faithfully adhered to the edict that bread was a sacred possession. Ben, however, offered me his bread. That supposedly made accepting it legitimate, but it presented me with a terrible dilemma. Of course I was very hungry most of the time and subject to the drive for self-preservation, a basic urge sanctioned among concentration camp prisoners. "Each for himself" was the norm. The step from human being to savage animal was but a small one. Yet those unable to avoid such a metamorphosis often could not survive. Therefore a close friendship, where the human qualities and values could be preserved in a small enclave, took on enormous importance. Such a bond was essential as a protection against losing all traces of civilized behavior, and with them a true sense of hope and reason for survival.

Although I did not feel such a bond with Ben, whom I did not know and who was barely alive, I could not take his food without an inner struggle. Even when he died a few days later and I did take a piece of bread I found under his mattress, I experienced a deep feeling of conflict. Gradually, under the impact of the large number of deaths in our ward—at least four or six every day—I hardened somewhat. For some reason, typical of the S.S. mentality, the numbers of the dead prisoners had to be inscribed in colored pencil on their chests to facilitate administrative accounting and identification before cremation. The cadavers were carried to a bathroom near the entrance of the block, and from there to the crematorium. No identifying records were kept of those who were gassed immediately upon arrival, since they had never "entered" the camp.

I knew how cheaply life was held here, yet I managed not to dwell on this. A strange feeling of immunity seemed to envelop me that was reinforced by my somewhat exceptional situation, my contact with Nora, my work indoors, signs that camp conditions had improved in recent months, and the growing momentum of the Allied and Russian advance. Prisoners had an opportunity to listen to the radio in the S.S. quarters and offices, and we rarely lacked accurate, up-to-date news. Some work details had contact with civilians.* The isolation was not as complete as it appeared at first.

Soon I began to explore the camp outside my block. Going outside was like an adventure; my world, which had been shrinking steadily, began to expand again. I had learned that officially one was not to be away from one's block during the day; and walking through the camp, unless on a specific mission related to one's work, was not allowed. But shortly before I arrived at Auschwitz life in the base camp had changed and discipline had slightly relaxed. There were fewer selections and cases of physical harassment. The roll call for the staff of my block, number 20, was held every evening in the downstairs hallway of the building with a minimum of formality, except when one particular S.S. Untersturmführer was in charge. He would strut up and down, looking us over, and make us practice "Hats on, hats off." My first explorations took place after these roll calls, when strolling around was not forbidden. First, of course, I went to look for Nora's block, which was just behind mine, the last but one in that row of blocks.

The last block in her row was the so-called Bunker, the camp prison. Stories of torture and killing there were commonplace. Partially surrounded by a brick wall, the Bunker was ruled by a huge, brawny, bald man, Jakob—a Kapo who looked every bit the executioner, an anachronism in this world of mass death by gas and ovens. Jakob was also in charge of the hangings—the punishment for those who had the courage to attempt escape or who were caught in underground or partisan activity sufficiently serious to warrant such a special death. These executions were staged on a square in front of the kitchen during roll call to make certain that everybody was aware of them. I felt fortunate that I never had to stand roll call where I could see these horrors. The story went around about a young man

*Hermann Langbein mentions the existence of a secret radio receiving and transmitting station in the "Bunker" Block 11 (*Menschen in Auschwitz* [Vienna: Europa Verlag, 1972]). I was not aware of it at the time.

whose noose broke but who was not granted the customary pardon and was executed the next day.

The square in front of the kitchen was also the Nazi stage for administering corporal punishment for acts of insubordination at work or in camp; twenty to fifty lashes with a stick on the bare backside, enough to cause horrible wounds that frequently would become infected and amount to a death sentence. I once witnessed such a beating, but only for a second, then I turned my head away. The same square was also the scene of Sunday afternoon diversions—concerts, variety shows, and feats of strength by Jakob, the executioner, who entertained by bending rods of steel into pretzels.

Further down the same street behind our block, on the steps of another block, I met a group of about ten Dutch people, all Jewish, who gathered there daily. Most of them had already spent half a year or more in Auschwitz and were very well informed about what was happening in the camp and outside as well. Their camp numbers were in the 20,000 range. They were skilled laborers, assigned to jobs inside the camp—sign painters, locksmiths, carpenters.

I discovered that Auschwitz consisted of a number of subdivisions. Our camp, the base camp, was the center. It was better organized and less crowded than the subcamps, like Birkenau, about five miles away, the site of the crematorium. Only a few months earlier a rather remarkable change—a relaxation of camp discipline—had taken place in the base camp. Previously, according to the old-timers, we could not have been sitting around outside as we were now doing, shooting the breeze. If you worked inside, life was not completely intolerable. The majority of prisoners, however, especially the Jews, worked on outside construction jobs. These nobody could survive for very long; they were a slow death sentence.

The Dutch prisoners knew little about Nora's block. I learned that from a block of the hospital next to Nora's I could look into some of the women's rooms, and if I wrote to Nora telling her what time I'd be there, we could wave at each other. Visits were too difficult and dangerous at that time, though I occasionally managed one by helping to carry the women's food in the evening.

Gradually I was introduced to the concept of organizing—that is, wheeling and dealing, including outright stealing. I found that I could get shirts and other clothing in the laundry, and shoes from the admissions office of the hospital, where I had had to leave mine when I came in. Bread was, however, the main currency, the symbol of power and status.

When I began to know more people in and around the hospital, I realized that as a doctor-nurse I was sort of upper-middle-class in the camp society. As a member of the staff I received a double ration of soup and occasionally some extra bread. The better fed I looked, the more authority I seemed to have. It was important to husband one's energy. I managed, following the example of my veteran co-nurse, to sneak a little after-lunch nap in a corner.

It struck me as bizarre to think in terms of social class in a concentration camp. Everyone entered it literally naked, as into life itself, yet somehow that did not make any difference in outcome. Besides national and religious attributes, certain personality traits like inventiveness and, ultimately, an instinct for survival affected one's position in this narrow, cruel, unforgiving world. I found that making myself inconspicuous might help me avoid trouble.

After about another six weeks I was given a bunk in the staff dormitory downstairs. It was a corner room, usually quiet and clean, a sort of enclave where I could sleep or read in my spare time. I found there was little contact between the people in the room. It took me a long time, maybe a month, before I got to know anything about the man in the bunk above me. Sometimes people would disappear and nobody would talk about it. It looked as if everyone wanted the utmost privacy.

Generally speaking, I had much closer contact with

people in other parts of the camp than with those in my room. But it was here that I again met Professor Samuel, who had diagnosed my diphtheria in Buna. He had been transferred to Auschwitz to work for Clauberg and Wirths. He never talked about his duties in Block 10, only about the past and his past accomplishments. He was a *Geheimnisträger*, a carrier of secrets, a very ominous designation. After about three months he suddenly disappeared. He must have known too much, or perhaps he had talked to somebody he should not have. We assumed he had "gone up the chimney." Even though I had developed a certain immunity to living in the shadow of death, events like this were a horrible shock and threatened to shatter the tenuous structure of relative security I had erected. My contact with Nora was without a doubt the cornerstone of that security. "If anything should happen to her . . ." was the unthinkable thought. I somehow managed to avoid such speculations most of the time.

In the late summer of 1943 Paul, for no apparent reason, was relieved of his job as block elder and replaced by Hans, another German political prisoner. There were rumors that Paul had been suspected of underground activity and put in the Bunker. Hans, was a quieter, more obedient administrator. There was no obvious change in the block except for a slightly stricter adherence to the rules.

At around that time a group of people who worked in a clinical laboratory, the Hygiene-Institut der Waffen-S.S. of Raisko, about five miles from Auschwitz, moved into our building. I would see some of them in the showers, one of our great luxuries. It was there that I met Dorus, a Dutch chemist and alumnus of the Technical Institute of Delft. The lab was an elaborate establishment run by S.S. Hauptsturmführer Weber and S.S. Sturmführer Münch with four lower-rank S.S. men, whose main function was to watch over the prisoners doing the scientific and ancillary work, including all the bacteriological and chemical analyses for the camps and part of the civilian population as well. The prisoners who worked there were either physicians or chemists. Several were Polish and Czechoslovak university professors.

Dorus and I became good friends. He was new in the camp, and I introduced him to the people I had gotten to know, especially the other Dutch prisoners. He was about ten years older than I and quite mature, with a philosophical streak and a very special sense of humor that was almost as valuable as bread. My relationship with him and a select few, the most important being Nora, became a kind of haven outside the Nazi grasp. It provided a precious sense of meaning in the face of the S.S.'s calculated attempts to render life meaningless.

It was a generally held belief that the Dutch prisoners' chance for survival in these camps was poor. Life had not prepared them for the physical and emotional hardships they were bound to encounter. Not so the Poles and Russians; their previous experience proved to be more valuable now. Most of the Dutch inmates succumbed after a short while. I met relatively few of them in the Auschwitz base camp, which did not usually get new Jewish arrivals. One day, while visiting another building of the hospital, I came across Dirk, whom I had known in Mechelen. He had been sent to Auschwitz from Buna because of a badly infected foot, the result of a blister. He was quite worried because he had been hospitalized for a week and his foot was not healing properly. He had heard rumors about selections and knew he had little chance of passing, should he be called up. He was emaciated and looked like what in the camp vernacular was referred to as a *Muselmann* (Muslim). That name was given to the majority of the prisoners assigned to long hours of hard labor, like digging ditches and carrying heavy loads, who had to subsist on the official ration: a hunk of dark bread, the equivalent of four slices, a bowl of watery vegetable soup, and a cup of surrogate coffee. Nobody could survive long on such a regimen. I knew I could not and felt extremely lucky for having found better work and a niche in this world without mercy. I tried to help Dirk by taking him an extra bowl of soup or slice of bread from the extra ration I got in the hospital or from a "prominent" friend. I encouraged him, suggesting that he try to get inside work as a mechanic somewhere, especially with the winter approaching. On my next visit, however, I learned that a selection had indeed taken place and he was gone. I consoled myself with the thought that he, having already lost his wife and children, really did not want to live in this hell any longer.

We had some selections on our ward as well, and with the help of my older, more experienced partner-nurse we managed to conceal case records and send those patients with little chance of passing the selection to the bathroom or other hiding places. In this way, even if we could not do very much, they perhaps had a chance of survival, or could at least die a natural death. These selections were both infuriating and terrifying. I just could not understand how a physician with a mere glance could dispose of a human life he had vowed to protect. Even in battle a physician is not expected to kill.

Some of our patients, given their poor health and malnutrition, developed abscesses where others might simply develop bedsores. When conservative treatment failed I would take them over to the surgery in Block 21, which had a small operating room. On one of these trips the doctor in charge introduced me to Karel, a middle-aged man from Holland, obviously in great distress. The night before, his right leg had been amputated below the knee. When I came to his side he bared the bandaged stump with a gesture of despair. He was running a high fever. But his mind was clear, and when I introduced myself to him he told me that he had been a broker on the Amsterdam Stock Exchange and knew my father well. He was depressed and hopeless, lacking the will to survive. I was abruptly confronted with something I had both repressed and feared—namely, the possibility that I might meet my father in this place and have to witness his suffering and slow death. I could not imagine anything more horrible. I went to see Karel every day for three weeks, until he died. We talked about the good old days, about my father, the eternal optimist—dapper, active, outspoken. For a while Karel improved, but then the fever and, I assume, septicemia recurred, and one day he, too, was gone. Thereafter I thought rather little about my parents. I just assumed they had gone into hiding and were safe.

It was during this time, in the fall of 1943,* that I again met Ellis, the medical graduate student from the University of Utrecht who had introduced me to the Zionist student organization where I had met Nora. He was a patient and was waiting to get some job in the hospital. It was certainly a peculiar place for a reunion. I brought him up to date on Nora's and my lives since he and I had last met.

With a sad smile, he told me that he and his wife had been taken prisoners on a streetcar in Rotterdam. He had tried to escape but was caught and sent to Westerbork and then to Auschwitz. His wife, Rebecca, had come with him, but he was afraid she was lost. He had been brought to this camp because he was a doctor.

I tried to cheer him up and told him I would try as best I could to help. We shook hands, and he thanked me for my efforts. I don't think we realized then how important it was to both of us to find someone we had known well in that other, faraway world. The next day, in the early afternoon on my way to see him, I came upon a horse-drawn cart filled with cabbages on its way to the kitchen. Few people were around in early afternoon, so I took a chance and grabbed one of the cabbages, stuffing it under my jacket. Ellis was delighted with that extra bit of nutritious food. I had also spoken with Dorus and with Pavel, the Kapo of the scientific division of the Raisko laboratory, to tell them about Ellis, a graduate bacteriologist. A few days later Ellis was transferred to the Raisko group.

Shortly thereafter I met Ed, another Dutch physician recently arrived from Holland. He was working as a nurse

*Recently I learned that it was the fall of 1944. The time spent together was so important that I remembered it as one and a half years instead of half a year.

in another part of the hospital, Block 9, next to Nora. I found that I could look into Nora's room from Ed's ward and wave at her.

One day, after having heard shooting for most of the day, we were told on returning to our bunks after work not to look outside. Nobody was allowed outside. Of course this only increased our curiosity; I tried to steal a glimpse of what was going on. The street on which we looked down was deserted. In front of the gate opening on the courtyard, between Nora's block and the Bunker, stood two or three trucks. Prisoners and S.S. soldiers were loading corpses onto the trucks, throwing them in the back like slabs of meat in an abattoir. The blood was literally running into the gutter. I watched for only a moment before turning away, appalled. I thought I had seen everything, yet apparently there was always something still worse. The story went around that a group of several hundred partisans had been shot at the Black Wall. Later we learned that the S.S. had murdered a large number of inmates suspected of participating in the camp resistance movement by shooting them in the neck. These prisoners were victims of spies of the Political Department. By next morning everything was cleaned up as though nothing had happened, except for red stains in the gutter.

Shortly after that event we heard that as proof of their humanity the S.S. were going to set up a brothel in the camp.* Its inmates would be specially selected prisoners headed by a Kapo, the madam. It was to be located in the building next to the entrance gate on the upper floor. Of course it was only for non-Jewish prisoners. It was never made clear whether this restriction applied also to the women. The brothel became quite popular, and advance reservations were required. Sometime later stories began to circulate about orgies with some of the important Kapos.

*In his memoirs Hess stated that the purpose of the brothel was to prevent homosexuality (*The Autobiography of Rudolf Hess,* trans. C. FitzGibbon [London: Weidenfeld and Nicholson, 1960]).

XIV

Not long after these events the rainy, damp fall weather gave way to clear, cold winter days. One day the chief of the hospital, a Polish doctor named Dering, a political prisoner, a bold, heavy-set army officer as virulently anti-Semitic as the Nazis, stopped to ask my age while inspecting our ward. I told him I was twenty-five. He maintained that I appeared to be much younger and hence could not possibly be a doctor. I swore that I was a doctor and that I was twenty-five. He did not say anything more and walked on.

A few days later I learned from some people in my block that I was marked for transport to another camp. I was horror-stricken and panicked. The idea of being separated from Nora was more than I could bear. I could not believe it; I knew this would be the end of me. Transfer to another camp would very likely mean loss of the position of doctor or nurse, assignment to an outdoor job, and ultimately becoming a Muselmann and then going up the chimney. If Paul had still been the block elder this would not have happened. I sneaked up to the window of Nora's room to see whether she could pull some strings. I also talked with Hans, our block leader, and with Dering himself, but to no avail.

After several days of unbearable suspense Hans told

me that in a week I was to be transferred to a very select work group housed in Block 12, the best block in the camp, assigned to cleaning the rooms of an S.S. dormitory just outside the camp. The work group consisted of only four men. I felt sad leaving the hospital. For me it had been a protected enclave with some sense of a future. In spite of all the reassurances and favorable reports about my new job I felt skeptical. It was a nonmedical assignment, yet, strange as it may sound, I was extremely thankful and relieved that I would be staying in Auschwitz. I am certain that Paul, with whom I happened to speak briefly during those days, had been instrumental in getting me this new job. He conceded that had he still been in the hospital I would not have been transferred.

The move to the new block was uneventful. I was the only Jew in a room with about fifteen others, all Poles, all "prominents," working in so-called important jobs like the kitchen and S.S. offices or barracks. Interestingly enough, we did not have a Kapo. We worked in small groups or alone and reported on entering or leaving the camp. The three others in my group were very pleasant and reassuring. The oldest, Pjotr, was a family man in his late thirties who used to work in the coal mines near Auschwitz. He was our leader by consensus. The other two were about my age and accustomed to working with their hands. They told me there would be plenty of food because the S.S. usually left their rations for us, while they themselves ate food from the nearby farms. Indeed, everybody in my room looked well fed and was dressed in new or custom-made uniforms.

Even though I felt out of place, I began to sense that what at first had looked like a disaster might turn out to be a blessing. I would be working in a clean environment, indoors, decently fed, and away from the danger of tuberculosis. Perhaps now I could take extra bread to Nora and make up for the food she had saved to help me. With these thoughts and with a sense of curious anticipation, I went to sleep that first day as a "servant of the S.S."

I had not been out of the camp since my arrival and had never seen the entrance gate and street leading to the camp's main street. This rather short stretch to the gate was bordered on each side with wooden cutouts showing a Kapo exhorting his men to work harder and in some displays beating them. I noticed that the gate itself was, not without irony, topped by an arc with a large inscription saying *Arbeit macht frei*. Every morning at 5:30 or 6:00 all the work details would march out through that gate in neat rows of five to the playing of a band, to return at 4:30 or 5:00 in the afternoon. On their return, S.S. guards would conduct spot checks or look at unusual objects being brought back. The four of us, under the "leadership" of Pjotr, walked with an S.S. guard to the barracks we were to keep spotlessly clean, three-quarters of a mile away, still within the outer fence or demarcation of the camp. The barracks was a brick building not unlike the blocks in the camp itself, but with more and smaller rooms and dormitories containing regular beds. I was assigned certain rooms. This meant making the beds, dusting, cleaning floors, and polishing boots and shoes. I took hold of this job quite well, though I felt like cursing when polishing the muddy S.S. boots. Still, this was paradise compared with most other jobs at the camp, including that of nurse.

Most of the rooms were unoccupied because the S.S. were away on assignments, and to be left to myself was an unexpected boon, a breath of fresh air. Only now did I realize what crowded conditions I had been living under. My awareness of privacy was even stronger in the bathroom of this building, which had one toilet in it behind a door with a lock. After a few days I found that some of the S.S. would leave bread in "my" rooms or come by with a container of pureed potatoes or cereal, part of their regular meal, at lunchtime—for fear of disease in malnourished prisoners, we surmised. I could work at my own pace as long as the job was done. Pjotr took most of the special requests directly from the S.S. and divided them among us.

I talked as little as possible with the S.S., and they with me. The idea of ingratiating myself with them was repulsive to me, and I must have impressed them as being very aloof. I felt that all they could expect was for me to do my job well.

Nora and I had worked out an arrangement whereby I would go to her block at a given time at the end of our workday, when the entrance door was open. The woman who acted as doorkeeper would get her, and we would talk briefly. I would take some food for her and some for the doorkeeper. We usually stood in the hallway while talking about the day's experiences or news.

On one such visit Nora told me that a Russian working in the block next to hers had waved to her, and when she had looked out the window he had exposed himself. She smiled somewhat strangely in telling me this and tried to make light of it. I cursed him and told Nora to be careful. She promised she would and told me that some of the women acted seductively to get extra bread or other food.

I conjectured that these Russians and Poles must be getting plenty of food, otherwise their sexual drive would be no greater than that of most of us. I had begun to notice a difference myself since I was eating better.

Nora said that she too had noticed a difference, although she didn't think much about sex. She also told me that some of the women had regular boyfriends. We parted with a kiss and a hug. I wondered briefly why she had even come to the window when summoned by the Russian, but not for long. Our relationship was far too important to let jealous doubts interfere. I was also aware of the tensions and need for distraction that must have prevailed in Nora's block, with all those women cooped up day after day and the threat of mutilating operations hovering over them. Nora talked hardly at all about this aspect of her life, and I preferred not to ask. But my fear that she might be caught at involvement with men like the Russian and subjected to punishment, such as demotion from nurse to test animal, continued to preoccupy and enrage me. The thought of these Nazi "doctors" destroying her reproductive organs, as they had done to so many women, made me see them as the most sadistic rapists ever. Before, I had been indignant but otherwise able to ignore the full dimension of these crimes. After Nora told me about the Russian, my awareness of this threat to her as a woman would become an integral part of me.

Shortly after the incident with the Russian, word got around that a number of women in Block 10 had had their hair shaven off because they had exposed themselves in front of the window, and it was rumored that they might be transferred to Birkenau. I worried even more about Nora. For a while the door to the block was kept closed in punishment, and I could not get to her to find out whether or not she had been one of them. I felt very agitated and angry, afraid that Nora would be out of reach or worse. Fortunately none of my fears materialized. Nora was not involved, and the scandal blew over. But wooden shutters were put over the windows so that nobody could look in.

One day Pjotr told me that on one of his trips to the laundry with an S.S. officer he had talked with a woman prisoner who knew some relatives of mine. He said that the next time this officer went to get his laundry I should go along. The possibility of seeing an acquaintance and perhaps getting some news from Holland was both exciting and frightening. A few days later I went as arranged and for the first time got a better idea of the layout of the outer camp and its immense size. Among the buildings we passed were stables complete with an outdoor riding ring. Of course prisoners were taking care of the horses. The S.S. officer stopped to see about getting some fresh straw for his mattress. Fortunately they had neither straw nor hay, so I was spared having to carry it back, but I did get to see the horses. They looked like thoroughbreds, and I wondered from where they had been stolen. The S.S. officer, noticing my interest, asked whether I knew anything about horses. I told him that I had been an avid horseman and had won some prizes. He seemed surprised and shook his head as if to say he could not understand what on earth I was doing cleaning his boots. No more was said about this. We proceeded to the laundry in poignant silence.

Both men and women worked in the laundry, but fewer men than women, and again the men were either Poles or Germans. About half the women were Jewish. One of the men knew that I was coming and told me where to wait while the S.S. officer went to get his laundry. The woman was indeed someone I had known slightly. She came from The Hague. We had met some years ago when my father, brother, sister, and I, with some friends, had skated south from Haarlem to meet an uncle and his family. It was a wonderful, typically Dutch winter day, a delightful outing, in stark contrast to our meeting in this godforsaken place.

The woman, Sara, told me that two cousins of mine were in Theresienstadt. This, of course, revived my worries about my parents. She did not have any information on their whereabouts. No news is good news, I figured.

The unusual nature of this meeting with a woman in this—for Jews—supposedly asexual world made me realize again, as I had told Nora, that ever since I had been eating better my sexual feelings and interest were beginning to reassert themselves after what had seemed a very long hiatus. I also became aware of the great impact that any break in the isolation from the outside world had on me. It alleviated my sense of doom, at least temporarily. Such contacts were as valuable as food, and even if they were secondhand when I shared them with Nora, they affected her similarly.

The isolation of Auschwitz from the outside world was almost total. There was, however, a noticeable difference between information coming into and going out of the camp. The latter was by far more rare, because it faced more than concrete, tangible obstacles. War news, usually up to date, did get through to us regularly from the outside, and it was not merely the Nazi version, since there were links to the BBC news. But giving information in the other direction, from within the camp to the outside, was a very different matter, for reasons not easily understood. That channel of information appeared almost hermetically sealed. Why this difference, and how did the S.S. succeed in this? Where was the barrier? There were daily contacts between prisoners and civilians, and some of these civilians were part of the camp underground. Yet reports on the situation in the camps, even if they got out, apparently had minimal effect. Nevertheless, the smoke and stench of the crematorium chimneys reached far beyond the inner and outer fences, or *Postenketten.*

One aspect that played into the hands of the S.S. in keeping the extermination process secret was its *literally* unspeakable horror, the daily killing of tens of thousands, including thousands of children. This made it difficult, at least for me, to talk to another civilized person about the atrocities. We had somehow learned not to talk about matters that would have such a deeply shocking effect on another person. You were not supposed to lift the curtain on a scene of such infernal crimes, on things you might possibly only whisper into the ear of a trusted friend. I felt ashamed when telling others what I had seen or knew to have happened. In a general sense, every prisoner became a Geheimnisträger, a person who knew too much, as in a narrower sense poor Professor Samuel had been. Because of his work with the S.S. doctors in Block 10, he knew too much and was killed. The members of the *Sonderkommando* in the crematorium also were killed to protect the secret.* Knowing too much implied a death sentence. The Nazis had an unexpected ally in this psychological barrier that extended far beyond the limits of the camps.**

*Filip Müller, *Eyewitness Auschwitz: Three Years in the Gas Chambers* (New York: Stein and Day, 1979).
**This apprehension of becoming a Geheimnisträger may have played a role in the disbelief of highly documented reports from a few escaped prisoners (Erich Kulka, "Five Escapes from Auschwitz," in *They Fought Back,* ed. and trans. Yuri Suhl [New York: Schocken Books, 1975]). These reports reached the highest government

Another even more astonishing breach of this barrier than my meeting with Sara happened at around the same time, during the winter of 1943–44. I was notified that I should go to the camp post office, where, to my utter amazement, I was handed a food parcel sent by Anton's sister Jopie, to whom I had written on my arrival in Buna. It contained powdered eggs, coffee, Dutch honey cake—things we hadn't tasted for ages! Nora and I savored every drop and crumb, eating even more slowly and more sparingly than usual to stretch the whole experience over as long a time as possible. The package also increased my status, since I may have been the only West European in Auschwitz to receive such a gift. How had it been possible to break through the impregnable barrier between us and that place called Holland, seemingly light-years away? It was another one of those miracles which proved that there are exceptions to every rule.

Another very special luxury came my way. Nora had succeeded in organizing a bed sheet and pillow for me and made the sheet into a sleeping bag. For the first time in more than a year my bunk felt like a real bed. When it was very cold I would wrap myself in my blanket and lean against the tall tile stove in our room to get warm before crawling into my bed. Later I began to suspect that this prominence had its adverse side, too. There is a Dutch saying, "Tall trees catch most of the wind."

levels in Britain and the United States between 1942 and 1945 without promptly bringing publication worldwide (Arthur D. Morse, *While Six Million Died* [New York: Random House, 1968]; Walter Laqueur, *The Terrible Secret: Suppression of the Truth about Hitler's "Final Solution"* [Boston: Little, Brown, 1980]).

XV

One evening in January 1944, on returning from work, I was notified to report to the *Politische Abteilung* (Political Department) the next morning at 6:30. The order hit me like a bombshell. The Political Department was the most feared institution in the camp, the equivalent of the secret police or Gestapo. Its members could accuse you of anything they liked and use torture to obtain a confession. They would lock you in the Bunker, and the next stop after that was the Black Wall. My friends tried to reassure me. Some of them told me of being summoned merely to verify a letter or address, nothing more. I informed Nora and asked her to see whether there was something she could do if I failed to return from the interview. I barely slept a wink that night, mulling over what they might possibly have against me: Was I being framed?

In the morning I went to the gate and, escorted by an S.S. guard, walked to the Political Department barracks just outside the camp. It was still early; the sun had not yet risen much above the horizon. I was told to wait in a hallway running the length of the wooden barracks on one side, with small rooms off to the other side. I could hear muffled sounds behind the various doors. Some sounded like beatings, screams, or moans. Now and then S.S. men would come out or go in. A few other prisoners were waiting with me and at intervals were called in. Some came out obviously in pain, only to leave again. I didn't know where they went. One S.S. officer had a brief conversation with another in the hallway, looking over what appeared to be official papers, whispering something like "treason."

Time crept by slowly; the light outside grew dim, and I realized it must be late in the afternoon. My legs began to tire, and I wondered whether they had forgotten about me, and if so whether that was good or bad. The suspense was torture. Finally they called me, and I was taken to another barracks under S.S. escort. On the way I saw a clock. It was 6:30 P.M. After a short wait I was called into a rather large room with comfortable chairs and a desk, behind which sat a young, arrogant S.S. officer. He told me to sit down facing him, gave me a writing pad and a pen, and dictated a Dutch address to me. I had some difficulty understanding him, but I did get the name and street.

He took what I wrote, compared it with a postcard, and said, "Ganz genau dieselbe Schrift"—exactly the same handwriting—and accused me of having given a Dutch S.S. man the card to mail to Holland.

Completely astonished and helpless, I told him that I had never had any dealings with any Dutch S.S. man, did not know any, and never talked with any S.S. except about my work. He feigned disbelief, and I emphatically repeated my protestation, whereupon he seemed satisfied and told me to go back to camp. I walked back all by myself and told my friends what had happened. I worried that I had not heard the last of this, but a week passed without any further news. Nobody, Nora included, seemed to have any idea of what this was all about. My conclusion was that they wanted to scare me out of any attempt to fraternize with the S.S. or possibly out of the job. It also might have had something to do with the parcel I had received.

I decided to try to find another place to work even though this one, as far as food and working conditions were concerned, was difficult to improve on. I talked with Dorus about working at the lab in Raisko. He in turn talked to Pavel, the prisoner administrator of the lab, and within a few days my transfer was arranged. It seems that somebody was needed in their "matrix kitchen," the place where they prepared extracts, other chemical additives for agar plates, and other food bases for their bacteriological cultures. Two weeks after my interrogation I switched to the Raisko work group. I kept my old room. Apparently they were not planning to get a replacement for me in my old work detail. Pjotr did not like this much, as it meant they all had to work harder.

The laboratory was four miles from camp, and it took us about an hour to walk there. But it was a pleasant walk, at least if the weather was not too bad, along the banks of the Sola River, past an agricultural station staffed by women prisoners, to whom we waved enthusiastically in passing, and from there through a little village with typically Polish wooden houses. Straight ahead, when the weather was clear, we could see the snow-covered Beskiden Mountains along the Czechoslovak border. In the cold early morning the sky was sometimes a beautiful red, setting aglow the fields to the left across the river. To the right, in the distance, we could see the chimneys of the crematorium in Birkenau. It was a glaring and dramatic contrast: on one side the beauty of nature, on the other the horror of the worst mass murder of all times. Perhaps I was predisposed toward seeing such contrasts. They reminded me of the first hours after the invasion of Holland: my bicycle ride home along the river Vecht, the blossoming fruit trees, the meadows, the birds, and the soldiers shooting at planes and parachutists. My indignation and helplessness both times were almost boundless. The contrast intensified the feeling of impending danger. On these early morning journeys to Raisko we literally and figuratively tried to look the other way, to see the beauty and ignore the monstrous evil.

The laboratory was a new-looking building with three

or four smaller ones around it on a four-acre area enclosed by a tall barbed-wire fence with four watchtowers. Inside the main building were the various laboratories on two floors around a large hall. An impressive stone stairway led up to the large hall and labs on the second floor. The building was centrally heated, a great treat in winter, and outfitted with the most modern equipment, either stolen or specially designed in Berlin. My room, spacious, neat, and clean, was on the first floor in the back; its large window looked out to the fields beyond. All the glassware was stored in closets; the counters were black and spotless, as was the red claylike floor. My coworker, a young Czechoslovakian named Bobby, had been doing this job for half a year and was able to teach me most of the routine. We also had books with recipes for each type of plate or dish, which made the work easier, though extremely tedious.

Bobby told me about the roles and personalities of the S.S. who came around frequently. The chief was Hauptsturmführer Weber, probably the most arrogant, suspicious, and occasionally vicious man I have ever met. He had neatly combed dark hair and bright blue eyes, and he strutted like a peacock in his spotless uniform and shiny boots. He was indisputably bright but terribly demanding, and had a violent temper. I saw him humiliate an older, highly respected chemistry professor for not understanding his orders immediately, by making him run up and down the stairs and then around the building in the snow. This professor, incidentally, was not Jewish. Weber was equally mean to Jews and non-Jews. To be sure, this was not a particularly redeeming quality; yet, even though a veteran Nazi, he was never overtly anti-Semitic.

The second in command was Untersturmführer Münch, very different from Weber or the typical S.S. man. He was friendly, showed personal interest in people, never deliberately humiliated anybody. He seemed oddly out of place in the S.S. Then there were five *Unterscharführer*, or sergeants, who were in charge of specific departments.

Unlike Weber and Münch, who were physicians, they were laymen. Our sergeant was an Austrian named Zabel, a mean anti-Semite who at times would be friendly and try to involve us in his schemes and at other times would hit or kick us brutally. He had the dangerous look of somebody out for revenge. I soon learned to stay out of his way, though not always successfully. *Oberscharführer* Pargner, the third in command, though of lesser rank than Münch, frequently preempted him; Münch apparently could not have cared less. Then there was Fuggert, who was in charge of an analytic laboratory staffed by two women, the wives of chemistry professors who also worked in the laboratory. The women were escorted to the lab by guards. They were housed in the same room as Nora. Fuggert was perhaps the most dangerous of this group of S.S. men, and something of a Don Juan. There was a rumor that he was carrying on an affair with one of the two women in the hayloft of one of the buildings. In exchange for her favors she was rumored to receive special privileges. I don't know if this was true, but he certainly was capable of it, despite or possibly because of his anti-Semitism. He was totally unscrupulous; if it served his purpose he would get you into trouble and then threaten you with extermination.

Klause was in charge of the warehouse and requisitions. Any requests for new glassware or apparatus had to go through him. He was an obsessive, slightly petulant, but straightforward man who did not give us much trouble.

Finally, there was a young fellow with a heavy Austrian accent, Kaduck, the delinquent of the group. He would get drunk, lose or perhaps sell his revolver, and get himself in trouble, and sometimes he told us about it. He could be mean, too, and play along with Zabel and Fuggert.

The prisoner work group was a highly cosmopolitan collection, a mixture of Jews and non-Jews from Poland, Germany, Czechoslovakia, Romania, Hungary, Holland, and France, about thirty or forty people in all. We also had a Kapo, Karl, who was in charge of the roll call when we entered and left the camp or laboratory. He had a green triangle, which designated him as a criminal offender. We never found out what he had done, but there were rumors that it was murder. His job at the lab was to take care of Weber's quarters, which were in an apartment above the administration building. Karl kept to himself. I guess he felt we were too highbrow.

I enjoyed the congeniality of our group. Most of us had academic backgrounds and felt we had much in common. I was closest to Dorus and Ellis, walked next to them on our way to and from the lab, and mostly had my lunch with them or with Bob.

During my first week at the lab, Weber asked me to make some graphs based on numbers derived from an analysis in the chemistry lab. I realized that this was his way of testing me, because it had nothing to do with my work and with bacteriological culture media. I worked painstakingly, using a well-sharpened pencil and ruler to plot the graph. Knowing his penchant for neatness, I was careful to notice that one set of figures had been left out, an omission I indicated on the graph. Later I learned that this was a favorite trick of his. Fortunately, I did the right thing and passed the test. Words cannot describe my relief. About half a year earlier, when I was still in the hospital, a young Frenchman had been similarly tested. He had shown me the graph he had made, which was responsible for his rejection. It was a little fuzzy and had a few smudges from erasures. A couple of months later I saw him again. He had turned into a Muselmann. That was the last I saw of him. When I was given the same kind of test I remembered what had happened to him and was particularly careful.

This new lab situation was somewhat of a setback in one important aspect. There was no extra bread and generally no extra soup, although the consistency of the soup we were given was better than the average. Also, shoes were a constant problem, especially in winter when the road was muddy or snow covered. They wore out quickly, and we had to resort to looking for replacements in the hospital admission room.

I found, however, that when we had to prepare bouillon for the lab we could keep the meat. For some agar plates we needed cows' or pigs' stomach extract, which tasted all right when boiled for a long time. Another source of additional energy was lactose, which we used in considerable amounts. One strange food supplement Bobby and I found when we were extremely hungry was dog biscuits. Zabel, who was in charge of the German shepherd guard dogs, kept these biscuits in a drawer in our lab. We would toast them over a bunsen burner. They at least filled our stomachs. During the summer, the S.S. had a large vegetable garden, which we would pass on our way to the warehouse. We could sometimes snatch onions, garlic, and tomatoes, which we would eat with our lunch. Also, there was a little storage barn filled with corn, which we roasted in the ashes of the furnace. On the whole, I managed to keep my weight up and stay in relatively good shape.

XVI

Italy had been invaded, and Mussolini taken prisoner and then liberated. On the Eastern front things were going very badly for the Germans. At this juncture they introduced a new feature into camp life: camp money. Depending on the job, we were paid in scrip, which could be exchanged for things in a canteen. The only item worth purchasing was a sort of tobacco called Machorka, cut-up stems and veins of tobacco leaves, the dregs. One could also get cigarettes made of the same tobacco. With my salary I was able to buy two packs of these cigarettes a week. They tasted horrible, so I always traded them for bread. I could not understand why anybody would give up bread even for good cigarettes. But to some a smoke was more important, even though they did not have bread to spare. This does seem to offer evidence of people's self-destructive tendencies, yet there was a striking absence of such overt, directly self-destructive acts as suicide. I knew of only one such incident, involving a boy in his teens who was in the camp with his brother. He was depressed and would not eat, and his brother could not console him. One night he ran into the electric fence. Perhaps suicide was so rare because the Nazis were ready to oblige by killing you.

A psychiatric ward attached to the hospital was overseen by a Dutch doctor, Elie. Its population consisted mostly of ambulatory or borderline schizophrenics. Elie was very conscientious and worked long hours to get his ward well organized and to help his patients. As a result, he spent little time with any of the other people in the camp. I never got to know him well.

Sundays were the time for visiting and talking with people. Above all, that was the day when I would try to meet with Nora. Sometimes I managed to get to her room on Sunday morning when supervision was not very strict. The husbands of other women in the block also visited on Sundays. We would have a sort of brunch, almost a feast, with some of the delicacies from the package from Holland. (A second one had come about half a year after the first.) It is almost impossible to describe how much these visits meant to me. To be actually close to Nora, to touch her hand, to kiss her, to discuss Allied victories, to daydream about returning home, to eat together—was the greatest source of strength. I had made it a habit to go by Nora's window every morning, just before starting on the trek to Raisko, and throw a stick or stone against the screen to announce my presence. We would talk briefly, wish each other a good day, and then I would leave in a hurry. Just seeing her to start the day was so important for me that on the few occasions I could not see her I felt deprived of something essential. I would feel less human, like a cipher, living in a world of grayness with neither light nor shadow. There also was the associated danger of being caught by a guard, and that made these times even more precious.

I spent most of my free time in the company of the lab people in their dormitory and used my old room only to sleep in and to store my belongings, few as they were, in a locker. One Sunday in March 1944, perhaps a month after I had changed jobs, I found that my good table knife, liberated from the S.S., was gone. I looked around and saw one of my roommates using it. I asked him to return it, not realizing that he was quite drunk. The room was occupied by "prominent" Polish prisoners with access to ample food and a fairly steady flow of liquor, largely vodka. He claimed that the knife was his, made a threatening gesture with it, and before I knew it came after me, knife in hand. I managed to give him a hard shove, and he fell onto a lower bunk. To have a Jew get the better of a non-Jew was too much for his Polish roommates. Before I knew what was happening I was attacked by eight of his friends—all strong, healthy young men. They tried to punch me; I gradually retreated toward the door and with my back literally against the wall threw some hard punches and used my feet to shove them away from me. In the meantime, somebody, I assume Pjotr, had gone to get the block elder. He came promptly, stopped my attackers, and whisked me out of the room. He suggested that I henceforth sleep in the other room, with the Raisko group. Once in safe territory I began to realize how much the fight had shaken me up, although, surprisingly, I was not physically hurt. The next day I picked up my stuff from my old room and moved in with the Raisko group. I never got my knife back.

In Nora's block there was a laboratory that used glassware and other items from our lab. This provided me and others with a legitimate reason for visiting. Such visits became almost a daily event. Münch was the one who organized them and did everything in his power to help make them possible. These arranged visits took on added importance because the closing time of the entrance to the women's block had been moved up, and as a result we could no longer get in without help after our return from work. In his official capacity Münch was able to arrange permission for us to get in and deliver packages. There were four of us who usually took advantage of this opportunity. One evening when we were waiting in front of the door I did not happen to have a package, and after brief deliberation Münch decided that I could not go in. I had not talked with Nora in person for almost a week and had been all set to see her that evening. Deeply hurt, I had to return without seeing her. I do not believe that I had ever before felt quite so helpless. Unable to hold back my tears, I told Dorus what had happened. It seemed as if I had gradually become persuaded that we did, after all, have a halfway decent sort of life, and even an S.S. officer who appeared to empathize with us, when all of a sudden I felt that the rug was being pulled out from under me and I was again confronted with the precarious nature of my existence. It appeared to me that, in that one brief episode, all the injustice and unfairness in the whole world had descended upon me. The incident unleashed my pent-up rage, my self-pity, and old hurts going back to earliest childhood. The only other time I reacted similarly was when I was thrown out of the dormitory in Mechelen, where I had ventured in search of food. Then, too, a reawakened sense of trust had suddenly been shattered.

Shortly thereafter our group had to move temporarily to, of all places, the Bunker, the camp prison. There on the second floor we were quartered for the rest of the winter, while new quarters were readied for us in another regular block. Many an evening we would hear Polish or Russian tunes rising up as if from the underworld, sung by prisoners in the dungeons below us. There was one woman who sang her plaintive song regularly before going to sleep; it was unbearably sad to hear her clear, beautiful voice through the silence of the evening. She sang not only for herself or for the people in the Bunker or for those who had died in that courtyard, but for all the victims of the Nazis wherever they were.

I met Vladimir, a Czechoslovak, through Nora. He was attached to the hospital as a nurse in the outpatient department and occasionally had to go to Block 10, Nora's block. He had been a professor of physical education at a Czech university, was not Jewish, and was a political prisoner suspected of communist leanings. A stocky man with kindly eyes behind black-rimmed glasses and a somewhat naive expression, he exuded trustworthiness. He seemed to have a crush on Nora, who regarded him as a good friend. Because he received regular food packages and had more than he needed from giving massages to kitchen and warehouse workers, he would sometimes give Nora and me part of his bread ration.

Greta, the doorkeeper, was forever telling me about Nora's involvement with other men, and expressing pity for me. She never mentioned any names, but her tales worried me. Nora told me not to believe Greta, who loved to stir up trouble unless bribed with food. She reassured me that her relationship with Vladimir was purely one of friendship, that they enjoyed talking about his home and about Holland. She said that he was not the kind of man who would take advantage of her.

I felt almost foolish and apologized for doubting her. But because life without her would be unendurable I hoped she would understand my dismay. We put an end to this squabble by making plans for our future. We'd get married, and I would finish my internship and get my license to practice medicine. I even spoke of moving back into our old house in Bloemendaal and starting a practice. I had always dreamed of being a doctor there. I could see us sitting in the garden or out for a walk, sharing the quiet of a beautiful evening, savoring the fragrance of the flowers and the salty North Sea air. Nora spoke of continuing her music studies, of seeing the world, of traveling to Palestine and America.

When we said good-bye I felt relieved and optimistic. Vladimir and I became good friends and had long discussions about the outside world, past, present, and future. We worked out detailed plans for "the last day in Auschwitz."

I had a dream that I have never forgotten. It had to do with participating in a strange and violent kind of water-polo. There was the immediate danger of drowning, but I somehow managed to stay afloat and survive. I did not know anything about dream interpretation in those days and in general did not pay much attention to my dreams, but this one seemed highly significant, and I took it to mean that somehow I was going to survive. It was as if I were saying to myself, "Don't worry, no matter how bad things are, you're going to make it." Sometimes I would daydream about returning home, arriving at the railroad station in Haarlem amid tremendous crowds of people, a band playing to welcome us, the survivors—a hero's welcome. The idea of not just surviving but getting special recognition for an unusual accomplishment took on exaggerated importance. I needed something more than mere survival, not unlike a childhood wish for something very special that would come true if I made a superhuman effort. What I felt reminded me of the ancient Greeks, who had their legends about Jason retrieving the Golden Fleece and Hercules having to perform impossible tasks to redeem themselves, becoming acclaimed heroes, and marrying the women of their choice.

The contrasts in the camp were unbelievably grotesque. When we came back from work and walked through the gate into the camp, we passed the block that housed the brothel. The women were hanging out of the windows waving at us as a sort of welcome back. Everybody cracked jokes about them. This scene did not look like a death camp at all. Spring had begun, and along the main street in front of each block were patches of grass with beds of marigolds, very neat and colorful. The extreme contrasts in themselves could be deeply disturbing. One was never sure what was real. There was always the need to believe that the situation was improving, that the S.S. would be changing its course under the pressure of Germany's military setbacks. But we also knew that for that very reason they might become more vicious and cruel.

The contrasts were all-pervasive. They were felt in our lab, where we were running a highly efficient institution to protect the camp and its environment from infectious diseases and performed routine clinical analyses to help cure people, while at the same time exactly the same people were being killed at random.

One day in the spring of 1944 Bobby and I received a requisition for a large amount of bouillon, and we told Zabel we would need a great deal of meat. At the time many transports, mostly from Hungary, were arriving in nearby Birkenau. On our way to Raisko we could see the chimneys in Birkenau sending forth great plumes of smoke and flames, which drove home to us the precarious nature of our existence and the incomprehensible cruelty of the Nazis. When we got our meat it was obvious that it did not come from any cattle or horses but from very neatly cleaned human muscles. Bobby told me that this had happened before and that the S.S. made this substitution so they themselves could eat the animal meat, which was very scarce. Zabel told Bobby not to tell anybody about the substitution or both of us would end up in the gas chamber. The words to describe my revulsion to this gruesome discovery fail me completely. We debated what to do; the quantity received was far more than we had asked for. Of necessity, we made the best of this impossible and very dangerous situation. Nobody discovered that there was anything unusual happening. Afterward we managed to bury the remains in secret in an out-of-the-way place, mumbling a prayer for the dead, a token funeral. This dreadful scene was to be repeated a few more times.* On one of these occasions a fellow worker, more curious and hungrier than most, came into our lab room, saw the meat and, exclaiming "I love steak tartare," took a small piece and ate it. He never found out what he had eaten. We did not tell anybody, not even Nora, until quite some time later. It was a truly horrible secret.

In addition to those already mentioned, three more Dutchmen became important to me in the spring of 1944. One was Jan, a non-Jewish political prisoner who worked

*Müller writes about how earlier in 1943 Weber and another S.S. man, Kitt, had come to the crematorium to examine the thighs and calves of men and women who were still alive and select the best ones, before the victims were gassed. After the execution they would cut off those pre-selected muscles (Filip Müller, *Eyewitness Auschwitz: Three Years in the Gas Chambers* [New York: Stein and Day, 1979]).

as a butcher in the kitchen. We met accidentally while walking around the camp. He was thought of as a rather naive and unsophisticated fellow, and quite troubled. I never could figure out his problem, except that I suspected him of being addicted to morphine because he thought I might provide him with drugs from the laboratory. He looked well enough, so I did not think he was severely addicted. Even though I told him that I could not get him any drugs, he gave me a so-called custom-made jacket, which fit me well, that he said was much too small for him. (He was at least six feet tall.) That jacket was important because it made me a part of the "upper class" that enjoyed various advantages. It gave me easy access to places where I might otherwise have been questioned or would have had to wait. It worked as a special pass that, for instance, made it easier for me to get past the doorkeeper in Block 10.

The second was Tom, a middle-aged obstetrician and gynecologist, also not Jewish, from Utrecht, where I had gone to medical school. This provided a special bond. He worked in the outpatient department of the hospital, occasionally came to Block 10, and knew Nora. He had been arrested in the course of underground activities.

The third was Dolf, who was Jewish. He came from Amsterdam and, like me, was a young physician. He was also assigned to the laboratory, and he and Dorus, Ellis, and I made up the "Dutch contingent." Usually on our walks to Raisko we talked about the past, our student days and adventures, which made the four miles seem much shorter.

In the early morning, when there were few requisitions in our lab, I often managed to take a little nap by sitting behind the scale pretending to be weighing some substance, holding in my hand a measuring spoon that in case I fell into too deep a sleep would drop and wake me up. On 6 June 1944, my birthday, I did this. I fell asleep, the spoon did not wake me, and Bobby did not notice. The next thing I knew, there stood Zabel; finding me asleep, he packed me a very hard wallop on the side of my head, cursing me and obviously enjoying having finally found a "legitimate" reason for beating me up. He went on for almost a minute, trying to hit me while I tried to fend off his blows. He warned me never to do this again and said I knew where I would be going.

When he finally left, I remarked to Bobby what an auspicious beginning this was for my twenty-sixth birthday! But about an hour later the news spread from room to room, originating in the administration office, that the Allied forces had landed in France. The second front had become a reality. I could not imagine a better birthday present.

We were all elated and hungrier than ever for further news, yet we also had to be careful, sensing how easily the S.S. could be provoked. They were walking around with very glum faces. A few days later Zabel was unusually pleasant to me, almost as though trying to make up for what he had done. He seemed to have become afraid that they were going to lose the war. Dolf and I tried to think of what kind of punishment we would design for people like Zabel, but we found we were unable to conjure up anything mean or horrible enough.

After 6 June the general mood in the camp underwent a striking change. As news of the Allied progress in France began to filter through, the end seemed in sight. The Russians began to advance again too, and the prospect that they might reach Auschwitz in the not-too-distant future was extremely exciting. Many an evening I would sit with Vladimir on a bench behind the outpatient clinic, where it was relatively quiet, and we would hatch all kinds of plans about escaping at the very end, before the S.S. could shoot us all. Escape looked so much more probable than it had a few months ago. From my daily walks to Raisko I knew the way to the river Sola. Vladimir knew the way to the Czechoslovak border and the mountains, and he spoke Polish. Making and discussing such detailed plans were among the most exciting things I did in Auschwitz. We were convinced that it was only a matter of weeks, or a few months at the most.

XVII

In the midst of this excitement, one evening after returning from Raisko I developed abdominal cramps that would not let up even after a bowel movement. I felt quite uncomfortable all through the night. I took my temperature the next morning, and when I found that I had some fever I decided to report ill. I stayed in my bunk all day, feeling worse as time wore on. When I had to stand up for roll call I asked one of my fellow physicians to examine me. Suspecting I had appendicitis, they carried me to the hospital on a stretcher, did a blood count, and in view of the leukocytosis and fever, decided to operate. A Polish surgeon, Boris, would do the operation; Dolf accompanied me to the operating room. When I was prepared and on the table they gave me intravenous Evipan, a barbituate. As I was counting and feeling drowsy, just before I went completely under the anesthesia, I grabbed hold of Dolf's hand and asked him to take care of Nora.

When I came to again, the first thing I felt was a slap in my face, which instantly set off a horrible dream or partial fantasy of six men sitting on top of me who, after first seeming to help me, turned into S.S. men trying to kill me. I felt that this was it! I had to fight for my life and throw them off me. I must have put up a Herculean struggle, because I managed to break a belt that tied down my legs and arms and throw off those who were actually sitting on me. Luckily, with returning consciousness I grew more rational. I told them that if they left me alone I would be quiet, and calm was restored. That taught me never to slap a patient in the face to wake him up. Afterward we all worried about what my struggle might have done to the wound with its big drain, inserted because my appendix had burst during the operation. But everything seemed to be all right, and except for some local pain I felt pretty well.

The first day I probably slept most of the time, and the second day, after a morning washup by a young Czech surgeon, Boris's assistant, I dozed off again. Then somebody woke me up, and there standing next to me was Nora with an S.S. woman. Somehow she had been able to arrange this. At first she was somewhat taken aback at seeing me so pale and worn.

She kissed me and said she had brought me a can of apricots for when I could eat again. I thanked her, amazed at her skill in managing. For the time being, however, I was just having a little water and intramuscular infusions of saline solutions to keep me from becoming dehydrated.

The S.S. woman stepped away to talk with one of the doctors, and I used the opportunity to reassure Nora. I told her that I was sure to be all right in a week or two, before we were liberated. She looked a bit doubtful, and said she'd be in touch via Vladimir, who would come to see me and deliver any message I might have. She also said she would try to come again in a couple of days. Nora's presence here was miraculous: a woman in, of all places, a male hospital ward in Auschwitz. To touch her, to feel her hand, her kiss, gave me the kind of strength I needed to pull through.

Nora had a knack for organizing. She was inventive and willing to take risks, and in the past this had occasionally caused some painful arguments between us. She would have been more readily inclined than I to disregard some of the newly imposed Nazi rules, for example, by going for a stroll in a park off-limits to Jews. My mother, who was a stickler for rules and doing the correct thing, used to caution me about Nora's devil-may-care attitude.

Whatever the pros and cons at the time, her talent for finding her way and her willingness to take risks were made to order for life in a concentration camp. She was not imprudent, but little would stop her once she had decided on a course of action.

I was agonizingly thirsty, but for the first twenty-four hours after the operation I abstained from eating or drinking. After that I gradually began to take some fluids and farina. I worried that I might not recover in time for the liberation of Auschwitz and the possibility of escape. We heard vague news reports that most of France, Belgium, and the south of Holland had been liberated. It all was going so fast that we expected Germany to collapse any moment.*

I continued to improve for several days, then suddenly took a turn for the worse. I awoke with severe cramps during the night and vomited, and it became obvious that I had developed peritonitis. I did not eat or drink for about two weeks and was kept alive through the intramuscular infusion of fluids from the lab. On several occasions, to my great surprise, Münch came to see me. To me this meant that, despite the rules, the Raisko S.S. were interested in and working to keep me alive, at least as far as Münch was concerned. Gradually I began to get better, able to drink again and take solid food. When I got up for the first time my legs felt terribly wobbly and would barely support me. I would go downstairs and sit in the summer sun in the yard next to the block. But climbing back up the stairs was a shock; I realized how weak I had become. I was reminded

*In Holland just before the battle of Arnhem, people experienced the same excitement (Cornelius Ryan, "Crazy Tuesday," in *A Bridge Too Far* [New York: Simon and Schuster, 1974]).

of Mechelen, where during my lowest period I had experienced the same problem negotiating stairs.

I regained strength daily, however, and the wound healed well. In the afternoon, around three or four o'clock, I would walk to a large grassy area with some birch trees close to the fence, the so-called *Birken Allee*, which also had a swimming pool with a nine-foot diving board. Like a country club. Ed and some of the other Dutch inmates, Elie and Tom among them, would gather there to discuss, or rather feast on, the news. I suggested we talk in English as a kind of dry run for our liberation by, we hoped, the British or Americans; it made me feel as though we were free already. Now and then, looking at the barbed-wire fence just beyond the pool and the guard tower, I had to remind myself that I was actually a prisoner in a concentration camp called Auschwitz.

The Nazis were not giving up easily. Hitler's reaction to his miraculous escape from the assassination attempt in Poland was proof of this. New transports were arriving almost daily, including a large group of Gypsies. They were temporarily put up in Block 10 and from there sent straight to the crematorium. Nora and the other women had been transferred to a block outside the camp, similar to the one I had worked in for the S.S. This was disconcerting because it meant that our daily contact was now over except for notes, usually carried by Vladimir, though Nora managed to come to the hospital a few times. Later she arranged for weekend practice sessions, at which I was present, with a small group of musicians in the camp.

A number of Dutchmen had arrived and were housed in one of the regular blocks. This meant that they were not earmarked for immediate extermination. I was both eager and apprehensive to hear about the situation in Holland. One of the new arrivals told me that he had known my parents in Westerbork. They had been rounded up in June 1943 and deported about a month later. I was stunned but strangely numb, as though the news did not really sink in. He also told me that there were very few Jews left in Holland besides those in hiding. The food situation had become terrible; people were starving to death.

We tried to encourage each other with the expectation that the end of the war was in sight. But I was not all there after the news of my parents' deportation. I don't know the name of the man who brought me this awful news, probably forgot it then and there, and did not see him again afterward. I held no hope for my parents' survival. I shut this devastating news off completely, did not ask for details, and somehow did not really mourn them at that time. I had tried to convince myself that they had gone into hiding and were safe; now finally that belief was shattered.

I could barely think back to the last time I saw them, when we said good-bye that October afternoon in Amsterdam. We knew somehow that this would be our last meeting. At that time in Auschwitz it was almost impossible for me to go beyond that point, to imagine their suffering, their removal to the Plantage Theater staging area, the train ride to Westerbork, the frantic efforts to avoid deportation to the east. Perhaps they had met their final fate in Birkenau. When Bobby buried the remains of the "meat" in Raisko and said the prayer for the dead, sometime before this "official" confirmation of their death, I had thought that it might also be for my father and mother. Deep down I had been mourning them for a long time, despite my surface effort to forget. I shed no tears as I had when I was prevented from seeing Nora for one afternoon only. I could not yet take in the enormity of this loss of both my parents.

I told Nora the news somewhat later; she took it matter-of-factly. Nora mentioned her worry about her parents' fate, but I reminded her that we had learned that they reportedly had been transported to Bergen-Belsen, rumored to be one of the better camps. For them there was still hope.

The closest I came to learning of my parents' fate was through letters after the war. Even then people were still afraid to talk about what they knew, and I was not inclined to ask. One of these letters was from Frans, an associate of my father's office for many years and his only non-Jewish contact at that time. Shortly after the liberation of Holland he wrote to my brother, Lex, in the United States:

The last personal contact I had with your parents was a few days before Wednesday, the 26th of May 1943. That was the day of the razzia *[round-up] when the entire area of the city to which the Jews had been confined was evacuated to Westerbork, a concentration camp in the northeast province of Drente. Imagine, all passages to that part of Amsterdam are closed off at 3 P.M. The bridges are pulled up so that I cannot get through to see them. All my efforts are in vain. When finally at 8 P.M. the siege is lifted, I manage to get through, but my worst fears are realized. A neighbor in their street tells me that they all have been taken away to a collection center on the Linnaeus Straat. When I arrive there I realize that all of them have already been taken by train to Westerbork.*

Shortly before this fatal day, Schouten, a friend with a farm outside Amsterdam, had offered your parents a place to hide. Your father, however, decided against this plan because he did not want to bring Schouten in any danger. You must understand that if they had been discovered the consequences would have been terrible. Many people who "sinned" thus had to pay with their lives.

As soon as I received a note from your father that they were in Barrack 55 I was able to send them food parcels. This was possible with only a few tricks. After July 20, 1943, when a large transport left Westerbork for an unknown destination, I lost contact with your parents. Soon after the liberation the names of those who were found by the Americans or the British were listed at various locations, but no matter how much I searched I could not find anybody.

Lex had also established contact with Nora's parents, in February 1945. Miraculously, they had been released to

Palestine in late 1944 and had settled in Jerusalem. They wrote about their last contact with my parents:

They lived relatively well in their room in Amsterdam until May 1943, when they were sent to Westerbork, more than half a year after we had been sent there. Nora and Louis were taken prisoner in Belgium in October 1942. First they were in prison, from where Nora wrote us. From there they were sent to Mechelen. We received several cards from there by both of them. In April we suddenly received a letter in which they reported that they would go to Poland. Nora wrote, "Louis as train doctor and I as nurse. We are full of hope, courage and will survive." This letter was followed by three cards from Nora, also signed by Louis, which arrived in August and October 1943. They told us that given the circumstances they were in good shape. They worked near each other, which seemed very unusual, Louis as a doctor and Nora as a nurse. They longed for news from us and your parents. The letters came from Birkenau, near Neu Berun in Upper Silesia. Our cards, which we wrote regularly from Westerbork, apparently never reached them. Thereafter we received no more communications from them. Anyhow, in January 1944 we were sent to Bergen Belsen, where no mail existed. From Palestine we sent them certificates for Palestine to Birkenau which probably never reached them. By that time Birkenau was very likely already evacuated.

Now I want to tell you more about your parents, Albert and Clara. When they arrived in Westerbork, as was the case with most arrivals, they had no stamps or documents to protect them against deportation to Poland. They would have been shipped out in three days if we had not been able to obtain a certificate stating that they had a son in Palestine. In this way they were able to stay in Westerbork for another two months. They also received food parcels from Frans and were able to survive relatively well. We spent much time with them in our little cubicle, which we were privileged to have because of Nora's father's work as camp doctor. On July 20th, however, the order came for your parents to leave on transport to Poland.

This was before we received the cards from Nora and Louis. You cannot imagine how terribly upset we were, but also how very courageously and calmly your parents behaved. They were almost optimistic when they said goodbye to us. Who knows if we may have the good luck to see them again? We cannot accept the idea that everybody, especially the elderly, who went to Poland, is irretrievably lost. We certainly do not give up hope on Louis, Nora and our son Bob. We count strongly on their return.

Although my parents missed the cards Nora and I sent jointly from Auschwitz, they did receive the first one I wrote on my arrival in Buna to Jopie, Anton's sister. In a letter from my father to Anton, dated 17 May 1943, I found confirmation of this. This is the last letter written by my father; it came into my possession only recently:

This morning we received your letter and Louis's card. You understand how uncertain we were about both and how pleased we were to learn this much. I agree, and my wife, too, that their card contained, if under these circumstances one can call it that, a certain enthusiasm about being able to help, with their love of life, their fellows in all the misery they will see and experience. When all this one day will be behind them, how strong will they be in their future life. These thoughts give us support and we hope that God will grant them a happy life thereafter. You understand, Anton, that we wish the same for you, your parents and your family. We all have learned a lot in these terrible times and draw on our memories and present evidence of the good side of humanity. We are both healthy and hope to receive good news from you and your family.

Anton, keep yourself strong; our best wishes also for your parents and family.

It really sounds as if my father was saying good-bye forever. He must have felt the overwhelming odds against him and my mother. He does not write about their future but relies on others close to him to come through this hell alive. I assume that this was written after he had declined the opportunity of hiding mentioned by Frans. He had made up his mind to meet his fate, I imagine, in the same way I had done briefly in Brussels after I realized that I was a prisoner of the Gestapo.

The very notion that my father and mother had entered this indescribably cruel world, so far unknown to them, ruled solely by the Nazis' mania to kill and maim, was too painful to dwell on for more than a split second, if that long. I could joke like most others about going up the chimney, but when it concerned somebody close it became unmentionable or unimaginable. The phrase "lost contact," as used for instance by Frans, invests most of these unspeakable circumstances with an infinitesimal ray of hope. With very rare exceptions—people like Pavel, the administrative head of our laboratory—there were no people of my parents' age in Auschwitz. Pavel was a prison veteran of almost seven years' standing, in a job with benefits not available to new arrivals. When he had entered this world, the gas chamber and crematorium did not yet exist and people were not yet being exterminated as part of the Final Solution.

Four weeks after my operation, while I was still in the hospital, the siren of general air alarm went off at about two in the afternoon. A bomb whistled overhead, followed shortly by a thundering explosion. Two more bombs fell in our immediate vicinity with the same deafening detonation. It was terrifying; the blasts came from the direction of Nora's block. Were these bombs dropped by Allied planes or the Nazis? The relief of the all-clear signal was short-lived; almost immediately a gruesome scene took place as the wounded began to arrive at the hospital. Covered with dust and grime, they looked like corpses, but on closer inspection they turned out to be alive. Among the victims were S.S. men. Oddly enough, everyone who could help did so without discriminating between prisoner and jailer. The structure of the concentration camp organization had fleetingly collapsed under the impact of the bombs. For a brief moment Jews, Gentiles, and S.S. were all the same. This leveling, remarkable as it was, lasted only half an hour at the most. The S.S. victims were soon transferred to another hospital outside the camp.

My worry that Nora might be among the victims, because her building was in the complex that had been hit, turned into agony. I checked all the incoming casualties with a sense of doom, fearing that one of them might turn out to be Nora. To lose her at this juncture would have been intolerable. When the last carload of wounded was brought in and she was not among them I was able to relax a little. Only the next day, when I received a message from her, did I begin to feel better. It had been a nightmarish experience. I had been through many violent episodes in recent years, but this bombing was one of the most terrifying, violent, and destructive experiences of the war. I also began to sense what combat or being in bombed cities must be like.

Among the victims who landed on my floor in the hospital was a prisoner who had lost both legs. He had been working as a tailor in the building that was hit. He was keenly aware of the danger inherent in his physical disability, but I convinced him that after saving his life and going through the trouble of rehabilitating him they would not send him up the chimney.

Not long thereafter a selection did take place. Everybody on the floor had to stay on or near his bed and then report to the S.S. physician and Boris, the surgeon, who were seated at a table. I felt confident that I could pass muster, or at least I persuaded myself that I would. The rest, the extra food, and the surgeon's reassurance had helped put my mind at ease. But when I stood before them I was quite scared. Boris said something about my excellent recovery from appendicitis and peritonitis, and the S.S. doctor nodded. I was all right. A couple of days later my friend the tailor was gone.

Again the cruel contradiction that permeated every aspect of life in this world prevailed: to be healed was to be killed, just as the slogan "Arbeit macht frei" on the gate really meant "Work will kill you." It was a world devoid of justice or reason.

Soon thereafter, having spent nearly five weeks in the hospital, I felt ready and secure enough to go back to Raisko. There a surprise awaited me. I had been at work for a couple of hours when Münch came into our room. He peered at me and said in a friendly yet serious tone, "You must stop now, eat some of this," and pulling a sausage out of his pocket, he ordered me to go outside and rest in the sun.

I thanked him, and he said something about gathering strength for the approaching fall and winter and whatever else might lie ahead. He was obviously letting us know, if we didn't know already, that the eastern front was steadily moving closer to Auschwitz. This, for a change, was an order I did not mind at all. I stopped working and went outside, looking for a sunny, grassy spot. When I came back, Zabel was waiting for me with a barrage of accusations and epithets, including *Sau* (pig). When he stopped— luckily he did not hit me—I told him that Doctor Münch had ordered me to lie down outside. He grumbled and left.

Münch appeared a few minutes later and asked me rather apologetically to hide in an out-of-the-way place when I rested outside, where I would not be seen so easily by others or from the road. The whole business was strange, an S.S. officer protecting me from his underlings. Münch was an unusual S.S. man, and gradually I learned more about him from others he had talked with and from himself. He was interested in art, and in a basement room he was modeling a head in clay. He had started on it when his wife had come to visit him for a few days. It looked like her. She was an attractive young woman who greeted us with a "Guten Tag" in passing but otherwise avoided the areas where we worked. Münch had mentioned once when he was in our lab that his wife was a cousin of von Paulus, the general who had defected to the Russians. As a result, both he and his wife had come under suspicion of communist leanings, and he was promptly transferred from the regular army to the S.S. in Auschwitz, where they could keep a closer eye on him. I tended to believe his story because he always tried to be helpful to prisoners, in contrast to the others, especially Weber and Zabel.

Because I had great difficulty seeing Nora even on weekends, after discussing it with her I decided—with considerable trepidation—to ask Weber whether he could find a place for her in the laboratory. I was quite hesitant about asking him and did not really know what to expect, since I had had hardly any personal contact with him. The war, however, was obviously going so badly for the Nazis that I believed he might be more inclined to grant some favors. So I gathered all my courage and one morning went to his office and asked to see him. I hated myself and the whole business. To have to ask that arrogant, dangerous man for a favor was agony. Yet I felt I had to do it, for Nora's sake and my own. He looked at me with his cold blue eyes and said he would think about my request but did not know of any opening for Nora at this time. It was a rather mild rejection. Nora nevertheless managed to come over occasionally with the two women who worked in the lab. Once, with the help of some of the others, who stood guard, we were able to be really alone for a little while in a large closet in the attic of the main building. It was a dangerous venture, but well worth it! She spent the day in the lab and did some work in the vegetable garden, sampling the tomatoes, cucumbers, and blackberries. It was one of those days completely incongruent with life in a concentration camp.

XVIII

After a very wet and stormy fall, the winter of 1944 set in early. The mud was hard on my shoes, and I had difficulty finding a pair that would withstand the elements. Nora made me a warm sweater, socks, earmuffs, and gloves out of wool from old discarded sweaters. We had a number of ways of sending parcels and notes to each other, mostly through people who could visit Nora's block outside the camp. The two women in the lab were another regular channel. Nora's participation in a chamber music group, which practiced on Sunday mornings in the camp, was our only chance for personal contact. On a few occasions I got permission to go to her block for a concert; the audience usually included S.S. officers, among them the commandant of Auschwitz, Rudolf Hoess. I did not pay much attention to him or the other S.S. as long as I could be with Nora.

I received another package from Holland and again experienced the rare sense of contact with the outside, free, human world, particularly my home. Each morsel of its contents was stretched to the utmost, both literally and figuratively. Home, however, seemed farther away again than it had a month or so ago. The battle at Arnhem had stopped the Allied advance to the north, and a newspaper gave us the Nazi propaganda version of the Battle of the Bulge.

Unexpectedly, and for the first time in my experience, a general selection involving the whole camp took place. We had to go to a building where we took showers, undressed outside in the snow, and, with our clothes bundled up under an arm, walked by a group of S.S. men. They picked out mostly those who looked very thin or emaciated, but not only those. I went through the whole procedure almost without thinking or feeling, and only afterward did I realize what had happened. At the time I was numb. One man from our Raisko group who looked rather thin and small but in fact was strong and wiry was picked and put in a block with all the others condemned to die. The next day we alerted Weber and Münch. Münch went over to the block where he was kept and managed to get him out. A very close call!

The lull on the fronts, at least the stopping of the almost continuous German retreat, apparently gave the Nazis more time or zeal to perfect their scheme of exterminating all Jews before they could be liberated. This return to the selection method was a bad omen. Yet in Raisko Weber and Münch saw the writing on the wall and were noticeably friendly—under Münch's influence, I assume. The other S.S. were also making some attempts to be chummy. And so our cry for help to retrieve one of us from the brink of death fell on receptive ears.

At Christmas, air alerts became more frequent, and around New Year we began to hear, mostly at night, the faint booming of heavy guns. There was a complete blackout on news about the front in Poland. We went about our daily routine as if nothing much was happening or anticipated. During the holidays some attempts were made to create a more festive atmosphere by giving us extra bread rations. We had become accustomed to the artillery barrages, which we estimated to be at least fifty miles away, and we thought that they would remain in place for the rest of the winter. Then, quite unexpectedly, on the night of 17 January 1945, after roll call, we were told to pack whatever we wanted to take with us and go to the kitchen for food. So the evacuation of the camp began. Nobody slept; everybody was busy assembling some kind of backpack with a blanket and other essentials.

Dorus, Ellis, and I deliberated briefly. Dorus declared that there was no use in hiding here. These bastards were certain to check every nook and cranny and shoot anyone found hiding. I thought we might stand a chance of escaping or being liberated by the Russians or partisans on the way. Ellis conjectured that there must have been a breakthrough by the Russians that took the S.S. by surprise. They looked scared and didn't have time to organize any mass killings. We were in complete agreement about almost everything.

There was not much time, and we decided that the chances of hiding in the basement or anywhere else were not very good. Also, we had an intuitive distrust of the Russians. They did not seem to attach much value to human life either. So we made up our minds to stick together and go along with the evacuation. Dolf, however, decided to stay and hide in the hospital.

We had no idea where we were going, but there was a sense of hope. The end of the war seemed in sight, and the S.S. were not shooting people on the spot. Actually, I felt exhilarated by the mere fact of leaving Auschwitz alive. All the plans for escape that Vladimir and I had dwelt on for so many hours suddenly became superfluous. Now if ever, I felt both extreme excitement and apprehension simultaneously. Of course, there was the possibility that they would march us into an ambush and shoot us. Rumor had it that the crematorium had been blown up, and in any case gassing did not seem a likelihood in view of all the preparations and the food that was being distributed. Yet it was possible that this was a ruse; one could never feel certain of anything.

I suggested that we rest for as long as possible because we were sure to face an exhausting march. We rolled up our blankets, tied the ends with strings so we could sling them over our shoulders, and put on as many shirts and sweaters as we could because it was bitterly cold. The ground was covered with ice and snow. Fortunately, I had a pair of good shoes and a pair of well-fitting galoshes over them, so my feet were warm and dry. I also had a pair of warm woolen mittens that Nora had knitted for me just a few days before, and a woolen headband over my ears.

As I lay down for a short rest I felt terribly worried about Nora. I did not know how to reach her. I went to the kitchen, where a line of women were waiting for their provisions—but no Nora. I asked whether they knew her, but none did. There was a general sense of urgency and frantic haste. I returned to our block so as not to lose contact with Dorus and Ellis.

We began to line up in our usual formation, five abreast, and became part of what seemed an endless procession of people moving slowly, stopping, and then moving again, gradually leaving Auschwitz behind. It may well have been a column of four thousand people or more. Other large groups were also under way, but I did not see them. We proceeded on the road to Raisko along the river at a moderate pace. When we passed the laboratory the S.S. staff waved us good-bye and wished us good luck. There seemed to be a strange sense of all of us being in this together. Some of the members of our lab group had been given a little cart at the lab into which they put their belongings and provisions and which they pulled along with ropes slung over their shoulders.

At intervals of twenty feet S.S. guards with rifles walked alongside the line of prisoners. From time to time, at a bend in the road, I was able to get a look at the length of this marching army of prisoners. It seemed to go on for miles. After proceeding thus for several hours some people began to falter, but they marshaled their strength and pushed on again. Those who gave up and fell down were summarily shot by S.S. men bringing up the rear. At one point there was a little brook or river next to the road, and a prisoner fell in through the ice and seemed to be drowning. I could hear the death rattle of his gurgling breathing through the water that filled his mouth and lungs. An S.S. man aimed his gun at him but was unable to pull the trigger. Another, bolder one moved in and shot the drowning man as if he were vermin. There was no "togetherness" there! All I could think of was to keep walking and under no circumstances to fall or sit down. We kept going on and on. Dawn came, and we were still marching. A guard next to me slipped on the icy road and fell on his rifle, which went off, hitting Ellis in the foot. I thought that would be the end of him, but amazingly, although the wound was painful and bleeding, he was able to continue walking. I gave him some aspirin.

The things we were carrying, like our blanket and a loaf of bread, began to feel like leaden weights. They became too much for Ellis, so Dorus and I took turns carrying his stuff. We talked very little. Everybody was just trying to stay alive. At daylight we finally halted in a little village and were allowed to go to a farmhouse to use the toilet and rest in a hayloft. It was so crowded that sleeping was almost impossible, but what a luxury to be able to lie down and close our eyes. It felt odd to be in a house that was neither a prison nor a camp, and the idea of hiding there occurred to me. But the S.S. guards manned all strategic points, and I was too exhausted to follow up on the idea. Perhaps three-quarters of an hour later we were told to get back on the road. I had been given a can of a sort of hash besides the loaf of bread, and I decided to eat some of it even though it was salty and greasy. I had been able to get water from a faucet. In my coat pocket I had a box with twelve ampules of a caffeine solution that I had taken from the laboratory some time before. I had come across it again when I cleared out my locker and decided to take it with me without much thought of its potential utility.

I felt a little refreshed when we started up again. Ellis's foot seemed better. He had unlaced his shoe and found his wound to be superficial. The bullet had lodged on top of his foot, stopped by the electric wire that he had used as shoe-laces. We continued walking in the same formation, Ellis between Dorus and me, for what seemed like an eternity. Occasionally the S.S. would let us stop to catch our breath. The shooting of people who dropped out continued at an accelerated rate. I did not dare sit down during the brief pauses lest I could not get up again. The bread I was carry-ing seemed to weigh at least fifty pounds. The sun was beginning to set again. Would we ever reach our destina-tion? I wished I had hidden in Auschwitz and waited for the Russians. I grew more and more worried about Nora. How would she manage this kind of march? We passed a group of women prisoners, and I asked whether anyone knew her, but no one did. I tried not to think of all the things that might have happened to her, but these worries would not go away.

It had become very dark. I began to feel drowsy and found myself walking half asleep, fighting to keep my eye-lids from closing. I decided the time had come for me to use the caffeine. Amazingly, within five or ten minutes I began to feel stronger and more alert. The mere knowledge that one ampule could have this effect made me feel better. I had a helper in battling my fatigue.

Our ranks, which initially had been orderly, in army fashion, had become stragglier, more ragged, and the dis-tance between the individual prisoners lengthened. There seemed to be fewer S.S. guards. We were entering a plain or open field when we saw a very bright light, a so-called Christmas tree, hovering high in the sky, the kind of light the reconnaissance planes used to illuminate an area. The S.S. anxiously kept referring to Ivan—the Russians—and, afraid of being recognized and shot, began to mingle with us. The whole experience took on increasingly bizarre overtones. Our exhaustion became more troublesome, too. When I looked into the trees alongside the road they began to take on the shape of houses, as if my wish that we were nearing a place to rest had become reality. I would come close to what I was sure was a house with lighted windows, only to have it disappear again. I realized I was only half awake, so I took another ampule of caffeine, and the mirages went away for a while.

There still was hardly any talking among us. We did occasionally wonder where we were going, but our main concern was rest and sleep. Occasionally we passed what seemed like farm families, some on horse-drawn wagons with belongings piled on top, followed somewhat later by a few soldiers and an officer on horseback—like a scene from Ingmar Bergman's *Seventh Seal.*

Finally dawn began to break, and somebody said we were getting close to our destination. Again strange things seemed to happen. I heard shooting and thought the partisans were coming to liberate us. Then the shooting decreased and receded. The S.S. guards, who again had hidden in our ranks, emerged and became vicious. I saw a guard hit a prisoner with his rifle butt to make him walk faster. It seemed unreal. I had been convinced that we were about to be liberated. The S.S. guard hitting the man in front of me must be a dream—or was it?

We reached an open area with large patches of morning fog. There was more shooting, and S.S. guards were pushing and hitting prisoners. Still, I did not know what was real until I looked at the gloves on my hands that Nora had made for me just a few days before. Those I knew were real, not a dream. I felt awake. We had come to a large railroad yard, and prisoners were gathering in small and large groups. I saw an S.S. officer standing at some distance between railroad tracks. I walked over to him and asked whether any of the women from Auschwitz had reached this point, explaining that my wife was among them. He looked surprised, shrugged, and told me to go back to my group. I was lucky he did not shoot me on the spot. When I returned to the others, mostly people of our laboratory group, there was more shooting. I suddenly felt or knew for certain that the S.S. were going to kill us all, and said so to Dorus and Pavel. Pavel reassured me and told me not to worry. He must have realized that I was in a daze. I don't know how long we stood there, but a train with open freight cars finally backed up on a spur. Dorus, Ellis, and I climbed into one of the cars. I sat down in a corner, pulled my blanket over me, and fell asleep in a second.

XIX

I am not certain how long I slept or how long we traveled. Nor do I know how far we had marched in the two nights and one day, but it must have been on the order of fifty miles. I would guess that we had been riding a day and a half when we stopped, as I learned later, near Breslau. It was 22 January 1945. We disembarked and again trudged along a country road through a little village. I felt hungry and ate some of the hash I had carefully saved. After half an hour of walking uphill we passed a quarry where I saw prisoners, their uniforms gray with dust, hacking away at different levels of the sheer stone wall. They looked ghastly, thin and exhausted. This was Gross Rosen.

Shortly thereafter we arrived at the camp, which was long and narrow, barracks on each side of the road on top of a ridge. We were sent to a barracks at the very end, somewhat isolated from the rest. As we passed by the barracks one of the inmates waved at us. It turned out to be Franticek, a Pole, who for reasons not clear to us had been transferred from the lab at Auschwitz to this place some weeks earlier. There were rumors that he was too valuable to the Russians to risk his falling into their hands. We ended up in what seemed a new barracks, completely bare, just four walls and a roof. We were packed in like sardines.

Later, when things calmed down a bit, we each had a couple of square feet to sit down in. Thirst began to bother most of us, including me. The salty hash was having its effects. Up until then I had not known that thirst could be even worse than hunger. We could not get out to the washroom in the adjoining barracks; besides, there was no water. My thirst was becoming worse by the minute. Finally, toward the end of the day, the washroom and the water main were opened, and water never tasted so good.

Nobody knew what was going to happen to us. Were they going to put us to work in the quarry or camp, or were we supposed to move on? At nightfall we got some watery soup, and then everybody tried to find a place to lie down, but there was not enough room. Fights broke out; people shoved and pushed each other. Suddenly somebody hit the top of my head hard with a shoe. I felt a stinging pain, and blood poured out of the inch-long gash. I used my make-shift handkerchief to stanch the bleeding. I was enraged. Who was the dastardly coward who attacked me from behind in the dark? Of course I couldn't possibly find out. All I could do was curse loudly. I did fall asleep, however, amazed by how much a human being can endure.

The next day we managed to get some fresh air by standing between the barracks and the washroom. At noon we were given some soup and bread before being ordered to line up and return to the train. Through all this Dorus, Ellis, and I had stayed together. We again got into the same railroad car, an open one, probably used for shipping coal. It was cold and snowed intermittently. I was glad of the open car because of the fresh air and the snow, which proved important in combating thirst.

There was a definite crescendo of horror and cruelty on this journey. We traveled for days on end, frequently standing still under the watchful eyes of the omnipresent S.S. guards. We received food, some watery soup, only once, when we stopped at a station. We kept each other warm by huddling close. Periods of wakefulness and sleep alternated. I lost track of time completely. We were all starving, and I seriously thought that if worse came to worst I could always kill myself by jumping out of the train and being shot, but I had not yet reached that point. At one of the stops we learned that several people had died in the closed car ahead of ours.

On what we later found out was the last day of this transport, 28 January 1945, Dorus discovered he still had a tube of toothpaste in his pocket. He, Ellis, and I shared it as if it were a delicacy. The peppermint flavor and the chalk made it seem a welcome nourishment.

The surroundings we passed through began to look more like suburbs, and signs told us that we were approaching Munich and Dachau. Even after all that had happened, I somehow still naively hoped we would receive some special consideration on reaching the camp, like any human being who had undergone a horrible ordeal. I felt that I deserved something, some form of recognition, for making it, merely for surviving.

After disembarking from the train on a side spur near the camp, we dragged ourselves through the gate to a building with a large hall. There we were ordered into hot showers. I don't believe a shower was ever more welcome. We had to relinquish all our belongings and all our clothes except our shoes. We were issued new uniforms and hats. It was shocking to see how much weight all of us had lost in the week since embarking on our long march. People who had been somewhat overweight looked thin, with their ribs and shoulder blades sticking out.

From the showers we were marched to a barracks: two people in a bunk, terribly crowded. Besides Dorus, Ellis, and me there were four or five others from the laboratory group. I learned later that the others had ended up in Mauthausen, Austria. A few yards away from us on one side was another barracks. Looking out through a window in the dayroom, I saw bodies being dragged and stacked up in the narrow alleyway. We had arrived in Dachau in the middle of a typhus epidemic, and people were dying almost in groups.

In our room there were a lot of people we did not know. Again it was a strange situation—not having the slightest idea what was going to happen next. On our third day in Dachau it snowed heavily, and some of us had to shovel snow in the alley between the adjacent block and ours. It was cold, but it felt good to be out in the fresh air, and we did not have to overexert ourselves.

To our great surprise Weber and Münch appeared one afternoon toward the end of the first week and compiled a list of those of us from the laboratory. They told us they had been able to salvage much of the lab equipment and glassware and were planning to set up a new lab here in the hospital. We were to help them. In the meantime they would try to get better living quarters for us. We were elated. At least we would have something definite to do— and there was even talk of getting us Red Cross food packages, which apparently had been stored away and never distributed. Now that the war was going from bad to worse, some of the Nazis, fearful of what might happen to them, began to identify more and more with us, the prisoners.

A couple of days later the lab group was moved to a less crowded barracks. Before the move, Ellis had noticed that his foot had become inflamed and had gone to the camp hospital; they kept him there. I went to visit him and, to my surprise, found a biology student from Utrecht, Tom, an old friend, in the hospital admissions office. Our reunion in Dachau felt like an omen that we would soon be back in Utrecht at our studies. This, like the food packages in Auschwitz, was another of those rare contacts with a world with which we had lost touch.

Tom asked us to come to his little station on Sunday afternoon, where he said he had a surprise in store for us. By Sunday Ellis was up and about, his foot healing, and we went to see Tom. We were indeed surprised to find there two men in S.S. fatigues who on closer inspection turned out to be old friends from Utrecht, Wim and Kees, both a year ahead of me at medical school. Seeing them dressed in fatigues of the S.S. was yet another one of those things that made me doubt the reality of all of this. For a moment I wondered who was fooling whom: were they friends or foes? When they saw my bewilderment they explained that they were in the underground and had set fire to the population register in Amsterdam. This list, which contained the names and addresses of almost a million people, had been one of the main tools of the S.S. and Gestapo in tracking down, arresting, and deporting victims. Wim and Kees had been caught, tried, and sentenced to death. But through connections with some Nazi VIPs their families managed to have their sentences changed, and they were sent to the S.S. stockade in Dachau. They were well informed about the latest news of the war.

As usual, when things were beginning to look up, a new catastrophe threatened. Several hundred people, including our laboratory group except for Dorus, were going to be transported to an outside camp in Bavaria, probably to make ammunition. As we were lining up in the central square of the camp we saw a couple of men walk toward us from the entrance gate, among them the feared Dr. Clauberg. One brave member of our group left the lineup, ran over to him, and told him that Weber had made special arrangements to have the Raisko group set up a new laboratory in Dachau. To our astonishment, Clauberg told us to step out and wait in a separate area. As if by a miracle, we were saved and taken to a block that was unusually clean and uncrowded. We had almost one side all to ourselves. Unfortunately, Dorus had been transferred to a different block with much worse conditions.

The other half of our block was occupied by a group of English air force officers and by Norwegian political prisoners. We soon found out that the Norwegians and the English were receiving regular food packages from home and the Red Cross. One of the most amazing scenes was played out every day at lunchtime. The English, very neatly uniformed and groomed—their heads were not shaved— would put improvised napkins on a table in one corner of the dayroom near a window and sit down to tea and sandwiches in proper English fashion. They behaved as if they were in their officers' club and never mingled with any of the others, in contrast to the Norwegians, with several of whom I became quite friendly.

At this time of relative calm and temporary security, I worried intermittently about Nora. What had become of her, where might she be, had she survived? I assumed she had, although I had no evidence. There were no camps for women that I knew of in our vicinity.

Walking through the center street from our block to the hospital I thought it was surprising, really, to be there all by myself in this rotten world, without Nora, and yet be able to get along. As a matter of fact, I was doing pretty well, had made new friends, met up with old ones, managed to get enough to eat. I found I could survive even without her.

At other times I would daydream of Nora, of our finding each other, getting married, and going home to Bloemendaal.

Besides the news reports that filtered through the camp and the radio reports from our friends in the hospital, the massive bombardments of plants near Munich brought daily evidence that the end of war was drawing closer. We could see the columns of smoke and hear the explosions. We also learned of the remarkable crossing of the Rhine at Remagen. Some of the Norwegians talked about being sent to Sweden soon through the Red Cross. These optimistic rumors and feelings could not completely blot out an insidious fear of what the S.S. might do in a final act of desperation. Another mass evacuation to nowhere?

XX

We were ordered to set up the lab in a wing of the hospital in March, and shortly thereafter we were given real cots in the hospital staff dormitory. Considering that this was Dachau, my life became luxurious. It was unreal, like a dream. I lived in a neat and tidy enclave, surrounded by horror. Only a hundred feet away people were starving and dying of typhus. The knowledge that the end of the war was near made this even more tragic.

Dorus, who had been separated from us earlier, also had caught typhus and was hospitalized. Fortunately, he was by now close to recovery. During our daily search for lice I had found an occasional one in my underwear. This lice infestation, strangely enough, was new to those of us from the Auschwitz base camp. In contrast to the other camps, Auschwitz, by the time I got there, had solved its lice problem by a variety of methods—among them the murder of thousands of prisoners who were so debilitated that they were no longer able to keep themselves clean and free of lice.

Ironically, the elimination of typhus took precedence over the lives of prisoners.* Of course, preventing typhus

*Doctor Entress of the S.S. organized the largest annihilation ever in the Auschwitz hospital, a selection of prisoners recovering from typhus. It took place at the end of August 1942, and among the victims were several nurses (Hermann Langbein, *Menschen in Auschwitz* [Vienna: Europa Verlag, 1972]).

also served to safeguard the S.S. Apparently a significant number of them had been stricken. Every block in Auschwitz had displayed posters showing an enlarged picture of a louse with the slogan "A single louse means death."

In Dachau there was not much of an organized campaign against this plague. The seams of the clothes we were handed on arrival were teeming with nits. It was difficult to tell whether they were dead or alive, and they were not easy to remove. I felt very fatalistic about typhus and stopped worrying about it. All my attention was focused on the approaching liberation. And circumstances seemed to favor this attitude: I had met friends and acquaintances from Holland, and our work in the laboratory was a farce. All we did was unpack a few glass beakers and instruments and store them neatly in little closets. Münch had provided us with a whole sack of flour. A good part of our time was spent making pancakes on bunsen burners. There were also some large containers with alcohol, which Weber, Münch, and Pargner, the Oberscharführer from the lab, who also had shown up, used to make drinks. If they could do it, so could we; I regularly filled some test tubes with their liquor, substituting an equal amount of water to maintain the level in the container.

A test tube of alcohol could get me a loaf of bread, which I bartered to get things done like having my hair cut, but only the sides. Here was another indication of our approaching liberation—we dared to let our hair grow, a previously unheard-of act of defiance. Weber, Münch, and Pargner left us to our own devices. They neither supervised us nor gave us any orders.

There was an unofficial relaxation of discipline. Almost daily, American fighter planes flew over the camp at low altitudes, dipping their wings as a form of greeting. The S.S. around the hospital would run inside and tell us to stay inside as well. But we ignored them and looked up and even waved at the pilots. The S.S. knew the day of reckoning was near.

At about this time Weber called Dorus to his office and

asked him to sign a statement that he, Weber, had always been fair and helpful to the prisoners who worked in the lab, a sort of affidavit to show to the Allied forces when the time came. Dorus had the courage to refuse to sign, telling him he had to think it over. I felt pleased and relieved that he never asked me. Pargner, who had been one of the worst, had also become unusually friendly. It was hard to believe the tables were actually turning. I had always kept my distance from the S.S. men in the lab except for Münch and saw no reason to change now. It must have been quite evident to them that I was not the one to help them save their necks.

I had gotten hold of a notebook and spent a good part of my time in the lab designing a home, as I had done in the prison in St. Gilles. This time I drew plans for a house to replace the one in which I had grown up in Bloemendaal. I did this, I believe, to persuade myself that what had happened before the war was part of an irrevocable past and that a new beginning had to be made. This feeling related above all to my parents, who had already become part of the past for me and were symbolized by our old home.

Once I had an opportunity to ask Münch if he knew what had happened to the women associated with the lab and to Nora. He did not know but mentioned the possibility of a camp near Berlin like Ravensbrück. He mentioned further that he had received a message from Pavel and several other former Raisko workers. They were in Mauthausen and had inquired about their chances of being transferred to the lab at Dachau. He told us that such a transfer appeared highly unlikely.

The weather turned uncommonly springlike that March of 1945, and I made it a habit to sit in the sun in an area between two barracks and doze for about three-quarters of an hour every day after our lunch break. No one seemed to notice, and no one bothered me, another sign of the changing times. We learned that American troops had reached the vicinity of Ulm and were approaching Nuremberg. At about that time Weber, Münch, and Pargner took us out of the camp to a storage area near some railroad spurs and asked us to help them load some furniture and belongings on trucks. They did not say why, but it was clear that they were preparing to leave for the south, toward the Bavarian Alps. Münch mentioned the Tirol, not bothering to disguise their intention to flee. While this was happening, groups of prisoners were still going out daily to dig trenches to stop the American tanks, a ridiculous and futile effort. Yet many of the S.S. guards believed that the war was far from over, that Hitler could not lose, and that they had a secret weapon that had been kept in reserve for the very last moment, perhaps a V–3 rocket. On a few occasions we had seen an aircraft flying at unbelievable speed high above our area and had learned that this was a Messerschmidt jet plane. We knew, however, that the Nazis had practically no fuel left for their aircraft and that the Allied air forces had the skies to themselves. The Nazis' belief that they still could win the war reminded me of the way I had felt in Holland before the surrender.

XXI

Just as the war was obviously moving into its final phase, we at the lab, all Jews, were given the unwelcome news that we were scheduled for transportation to an unknown destination. This move was allegedly connected with an exchange of prisoners arranged by the Red Cross via Switzerland. We were to leave Dachau in two or three days. We tried to think of how we could possibly avoid this transport. We felt fairly good about our present situation in Dachau and knew from bitter experience the hardships and danger attendant on any change or relocation, especially now that the end of the war and freedom appeared so near.

There was a general sense of upheaval in the camp. Transports from other camps had come into Dachau during the past week. Many of the people looked exhausted, as we had when we had arrived here. There was talk of a general evacuation of Dachau. But why should we, all Jews, be the first ones to leave? The aura surrounding this transport was ominous.

We decided to talk to Münch. He shared our reluctance to go on another transport to nowhere and offered some possible or impossible plans for escape. One was that he would take us through the gate and then provide us with S.S. uniforms. But it was not clear how even in S.S. uniforms we could get away and into Switzerland. We decided that we would probably stand a much better chance if we went with the transport and later escaped in the mountains, closer to Switzerland. He said he planned on going south into the mountains toward the Tirol and would keep an eye on us. To prove his good will, he gave us a revolver and ammunition, in case we had to shoot our way out. He shook hands with each of us and wished us early freedom. That was the last I saw of him.

In the meantime, we did not know what to do with the gun. What a bizarre situation—prisoners in Dachau with a loaded gun! After the initial excitement wore off the gun became more of a liability than an asset, and we looked for a secure hiding place. We pried a floorboard loose, wrapped the gun in paper, slid it under the board, and with a sense of relief nailed the board back in place.

The transport was to leave the next day, 26 April 1945. We woke up early and with a new sense of doom got our few belongings together and joined a group of several hundred prisoners in the *Appellplatz*, the main camp's assembly area. As we were assembling, the air alarm went off, and planes began to bomb and strafe what we took to be the railroad tracks leading to the camp. They must have spotted us and the waiting train. To our relief the transport was canceled, and our hope grew that we might be liberated before they tried to ship us out again.

Dorus was still extremely weak from his bout with typhus, and we feared that should we attempt to escape he would be unable to keep up with us. We decided to put off any action until we had figured out how we could protect him. One plan was to have him readmitted to the hospital.

Two days later we were again ordered to assemble for transport. Apparently, the tracks had been repaired. Ellis had "liberated" ten sleeping tablets. But we had not succeeded in our attempt to have Dorus readmitted to the hospital; the chief, himself a prisoner, claimed there were no beds available. In a desperate attempt to force his readmission we suggested to Dorus that he take the ten sleeping tablets. We were certain it was not a dangerous dose but that it would put him to sleep for quite a while. It did, and when he was semiconscious we carried him back to the hospital. They could not refuse him. We pretended he had collapsed from weakness during the lineup. Ellis and I did not leave until we saw him in bed and well taken care of. As we later learned from him, he slept for about twenty-four hours and woke up just a few hours before Dachau was liberated.

Unfortunately, Ellis and I were not to witness this unbelievable event. Instead, shortly after we had seen Dorus put to bed we returned to the central square and about an hour later were marched to a train with regular passenger cars. Some of our guards were older army soldiers, not S.S. They let us walk outside the cars after we had "reserved" our seats in a first-class compartment. To our further surprise we were each given a Red Cross package with cheese, canned meat, and crackers. This seemed to point to the possibility that the transport might in fact be going to Austria or even Switzerland.

Night fell and we still had not left, so we bedded down as best as possible, two people per bench and two in the luggage net above. The next morning we finally began to move. The scenery changed gradually from flat countryside to lush green, rolling hills. Later that morning we stopped at a neat, clean station in more mountainous terrain, where we were allowed to step out on the platform. Actually, we just went without asking permission, and the guards did not stop us. I even walked a little further along the train without any guard interfering. Most of the others stayed in the train, however. Some of the railroad employees on the platform talked to us; one said he had heard that peace negotiations had started and the war would be over very soon. I had difficulty believing this because of the many rumors that had proved false. The whole idea that I might in fact survive, be free again, was far too precarious to accept without more concrete evidence. Nevertheless, with all this excitement in the air I ate a whole wedge of cheese instead of dividing it into little portions to spread the pleasure over a longer time. It is hard to imagine the sense of utter and reckless abandon such indulgence conveyed. I simply had to express my exhilaration over this news by letting down my guard, even if just for a moment.

The train pulled out of the station shortly. The scenery became more and more beautiful as we continued southward. We saw traffic on a road near the tracks, mostly military vehicles but also soldiers on foot and people on bicycles. It did not look like a general retreat. Again I thought about escaping. Before we had started on this transport I had obtained a good warm civilian overcoat, although it had two patches of striped uniform material stitched on the back. These could be removed. I also had a civilian cap with no markings on it. Ellis had a similar outfit. But it had seemed too risky to make a run for it or hide in the station where we had stopped, and it was too dangerous to jump from the fast-moving train in broad daylight. Anyhow, we talked about it and decided to wait for a better opportunity.

After a few more stops, at about 2 P.M., we arrived in Seefeld, just across the Austrian border. The guards said the plan was to walk from there to Innsbruck. The tracks were supposedly destroyed, but we assumed the real reason was that the Austrian authorities were stalling because they did not want to be compromised by the presence of hundreds of prisoners, many of them ill with typhus and high fever.

The guards escorted us into a large meadow near the station where we could rest in the sun, while the leader, an S.S. officer, discussed his plans with the local authorities. A couple of hours later word was passed that we would march toward Innsbruck. Again we were escorted by guards. We formed a very ragged column of dismal-looking people. Many fell by the wayside, exhausted and ill. However, in this neat-looking town, with natives staring at us and shaking their heads but not daring to do anything to help us, the guards, afraid of the townspeople's reaction, were not shooting anybody. Ellis and I, joined by some others, stopped to put the sickest people in a barn next to the station. Some of the station personnel said they would care for them and get a doctor. Then the column started toward Innsbruck. The sky turned gray, and it began to snow a little as we slowly climbed up the narrow dirt road. Gradually it grew dark, and we stopped at a farm, where some of us were put up for the night. The farmer showed us to his hayloft and gave us milk and potatoes. Of course we were not left unattended; a guard watched us but did not dare to bother anybody. I could smell freedom in the fresh mountain air and went to sleep knowing that our nightmare would soon be over.

On awakening the next morning this sense of rebirth intensified. I was up with the dawn and looked around; everything was quiet, and even the guard seemed to be dozing. I got up, stretched, and walked outside. The most spectacular view awaited me. In front of me, bathed in the early morning light, were the Bavarian Alps, covered with a fresh layer of spring snow and hues of sparkling red, yellow, and white. The Zugspitze and the Karwendel Mountains showed themselves in their full morning glory. Because the farm was fairly high up, the panorama was fantastic, but the taste of freedom was what made this a truly moving, almost religious experience for me. I was standing on the threshold of liberation.

My reverie did not last long; once again we were herded together and, to our surprise, returned to Seefeld. Ellis and I talked with some of the others about what that might mean. We did not feel good about it. We assumed that the Austrians did not want us and had persuaded the S.S. to take us back across the border to Germany. In Seefeld we were again put on a train, this time in open freight cars. After several hours the train began to move.

When we came to the border near Scharnitz, two of the people in our car jumped out and ran into the woods, about four hundred yards away. They crossed the open fields between the track and the woods, and nobody shot at them. I envied their daring. One of them was the same fellow who had run up to Clauberg in Dachau and saved us from being transported. I felt more and more worried about what they were going to do with us and where they might be taking us. The very fact that the war was practically over and liberation at hand only intensified these ominous forebodings. The train moved along slowly and after a little while stopped near a bend in a partly dried-out riverbed, the Isar. We were told to get out and were rounded up on the riverbank. When I asked one of the guards the reason for this stop he merely said to wait till dark.

I knew we were trapped and in mortal danger. The S.S., true to their image, would exterminate all Jews to the very last man. I tried to sneak out of the roundup along the riverbank and take cover in some bushes, but every time I moved a guard would notice me and threaten to shoot. After a while, feeling terrified and trapped, I gave up.

At dusk snow began to fall. I found a dry, shallow brook bed, and when I covered myself with the blanket I carried with me it made a suitable lair. Ellis and two other laboratory workers followed my example. Strangely enough, I felt somewhat safer, like a soldier in a foxhole. The blanket, soon covered with snow, was excellent camouflage, especially when it grew dark. It seemed we were lying there for hours. I dozed off but was rudely awakened by the sound of shooting and bullets whistling over my head.

I remained motionless, close to the ground. After about twenty minutes, when all was silent, I crawled out of the hole to take a look.

When I crawled toward the road up the riverbank I found to my amazement that there was no one left. No S.S. guards. They had fled. I ran back to tell Ellis that we were free. We packed our few belongings, including our blankets, and began running in the dark toward the road. We did not dare to look back; it was too dark to see, anyhow. Ernst, a chemist from the lab, and Max, a general handyman, joined us.

I could not believe we were our own masters, that nobody was telling us what to do. When we got to the road we had no clear idea which way to turn. To the right, south, or the left, north? Looking around we spotted a little cabin some distance away in a snow-covered field, a little way up the mountain. The door was unlocked. It was partly filled with hay, a perfect resting place for this snowy, cold night. It was not long before we and three others who had survived the gunfire lay down and dozed off.

Perhaps four hours later we were awakened by a flashlight shining in our faces and ordered in German to get out. I could not believe my eyes, but there they were: retreating German soldiers who had followed our tracks.

With their guns at our backs, they herded us toward the road again and said that they needed us to build a roadblock. They never gave up. We walked down the same road, this time heading south, surrounded by the soldiers. It began to grow lighter. To our right was the river and to our left the railroad and the wooded mountain slopes. I felt more frustrated, if that was possible, than when I was driven into the Gestapo building in Brussels almost three years before. But this time I somehow knew I was going to escape. Having felt freedom just a few minutes before, I could not let it slip away like this.

I seized my chance intuitively when somebody in front of me tried to run away to the right and distracted the soldiers. I jumped to the left and ran with all the strength I could gather into the nearby woods. They fired shots at me, but in the dark, amid the trees, we—Ellis, Ernst, and Max had promptly joined me—stood a good chance. We kept running up the mountain, straight up and fast, as though defying the force of gravity.

I kept encouraging the others to keep it up, and I knew

we had never felt stronger. To feel again a sense of control over my own destiny after all these years of seeing it slip away, at first gradually, then almost completely—and finally a few hours ago to regain and lose this most precious treasure, then to find this chance to retrieve it and make the most of it—served to mobilize every particle of strength in my body. After climbing about six hundred feet in fifteen minutes we stopped, panting heavily. Everything was quiet. We were safe again, and we began making plans to ensure our freedom now and forever.

XXII

My love of the mountains goes back to my childhood and youth and the many vacations I had spent in them. I felt confident about how to proceed in this terrain, and my intuitive response inspired Ellis, Ernst, and Max. We decided to climb as high as we could and then turn north along the ridge, toward where the front should be. We did not think we would run into any more German troops if we stayed out of view of the road, up high in the mountains.

We continued our climb slowly and steadily until we reached a narrow path leading north, exactly where we wanted to go. It seemed made to order. The path wound through the upper reaches of the pinewood near the timberline. By now it was full daylight. After several hours we came to the site of a stone slide. Not only did we have to traverse a steep slope of loose stones, there was the additional risk of being seen from the road below. I went first and found that the stones held as long as I stepped carefully and rapidly to avoid being seen. Ellis and Max followed with no problem, but Ernst froze a third of the way across, clinging to a wall of loose stones above him, in sight of the road below. No amount of encouragement could get him to move. We were paralyzed with fear of being discovered and tried desperately to help him by whispering instructions.

Finally, after what seemed like hours, he began to move again quite fast, loosening some rocks that thundered down the slope, but he made it. We moved on quickly, worried lest somebody had seen or heard us. Nothing happened, and we walked steadily ahead. About four o'clock in the afternoon snow began to fall again. In the distance we could hear the booms of heavy artillery, which meant that we were going in the right direction. The Allied forces must be near.

An hour later, a few feet above the path, we noticed a square, rooflike structure protruding slightly above the ground. On closer inspection we saw that it served as the cover of a six-foot-by-six-foot dugout with wooden seats along the wall. We all felt that this was a godsend, a shelter for the night. We cut some hemlock branches to make the roof reasonably waterproof. We also put some on the floor to make it drier, so we could lie down and stretch our tired legs. Max still had a loaf of bread, which he shared for our evening meal, and we drank melted snow to wash it down.

Just as we were dozing off after this sumptuous meal I heard some footsteps outside; my heart jumped. Not again! I saw two pairs of German army boots through the opening of our shelter, two German soldiers. Were we prisoners again? I could not believe it!

Max and Ernst, both from Austria, spoke to them in Austrian German. They told us the front was only six miles away and that they were on their way home across the mountains. They wished us a good day, slung their rifles over their shoulders, and moved on. What a tremendous relief. After they left, one of us went outside to erase the tracks.

We could now hear the boom of the guns more clearly, and shortly thereafter there was an explosion when a grenade hit. I had taken a small clock from the laboratory with me, thinking it might come in handy, and now used it to time the interval between the two booms to give us some idea of how far away the guns were. The second boom was very close in the valley below us. We figured they could not be much more than a few miles away. After that game we tried to sleep, more or less successfully. I could hardly imagine any situation more exciting and suspenseful than the four of us sitting high in the mountains waiting for the moment of liberation we had been dreaming about for so many years, each in a uniquely personal way. But we were dead tired, which took the edge off our anxious anticipation and enabled us to nap a little. Our body heat kept the small space pretty warm.

When I awoke and looked outside, everything was gray, but the sun was up, although I could not see it in the ten-foot radius the fog allowed. I could hear some distinctive sound from the valley, a kind of rattling and grinding noise. I told the others I would descend carefully and return to let them know what was what, but they decided to come with me. We walked down the mountain silently, like Indians. In twenty minutes we broke through the clouds and could see the road clearly. On it were dark objects that we knew were tanks. As we came closer we could make out white stars on every vehicle. At first I was uncertain whether the star was not perhaps the symbol of the Russian army. We were still afraid of what the Russians might do with us. Sneaking closer, we could hear English being spoken. At that, nothing could stop us. We ran the last hundred feet toward them. Ellis was the first to reach a jeep and a half-track. We had made it! We shook hands and embraced the Americans. They gave us cigarettes and chocolate bars and told us to go to a nearby village, Mittenwald, take possession of any house we liked, and make ourselves comfortable.

XXIII

And so, on 1 May 1945, we reentered the world we had left so very long ago, a world with which, except for a few precious moments, we had had no direct or tangible connection for years, and to which there had been only the faintest chance of ever returning. Now that this chance had materialized, I was in a daze. I suppose that is how the first astronauts must have felt when they returned to this side of the moon and reestablished contact with the earth, then came back to it. Very slowly I began to realize that I was actually free, my own master, once again a real person who did not need to fear that any moment might be the last.

When the four of us, unshaven and haggard from our last almost sleepless four days of captivity, entered Mittenwald, we must have been a sight to behold. Every house had a white sheet hanging out of a window to signal surrender. We knocked on the door of one of the first houses we came to and found a group of people sitting around a large table drinking coffee in a sort of live-in kitchen. They invited us to join them and offered us coffee and cookies. They did not have to ask twice. They told us that after a brief shelling the village had been abandoned by the German troops, who had fled south just a few hours earlier. The villagers were still shaken.

After half an hour of small talk we decided to move on to look for a place to stay and rest. We spotted a beautiful chalet up the mountain slope overlooking the village and walked up to it. Ellis rang the doorbell and a maid answered, opening the door just a little. He told her in his best German that we were looking for accommodations. She looked us over and told us that no rooms were available. We asked to see the owner. He appeared and, realizing he had no choice, let us in.

We introduced ourselves as two physicians, a chemist, and a businessman, and shook hands. The owner called his wife, who immediately offered to ready a room and put four beds in it. While she and the maid went off to do so, we and the owner, Karl, sat down in comfortable chairs in the large central hall, a two-story-high room with a concert grand piano in the center. Ernst could not control himself, sat down, touched the keys, tentatively at first, and then proceeded to play some Bach and Beethoven, tears running down his cheeks. Deeply moved and feeling more serene, I began to believe that I was no longer in danger, that I was safe and needed no longer fear extermination.

Karl was a tall, thin, slightly balding man, dressed in a neat brown business suit and eager to give the impression of a decent family man with an attractive wife and two young children. I could sense his anxiety over what would become of them. He was not very curious about our fate during the war, and none of us was ready to volunteer any information. Our conversation was limited to the immediate present and future. The fact that three of us were professionals seemed to reassure him. In trying to explain the maid's reluctance to admit us, he told us stories of looting and rapes by Russians and former prisoners. He volunteered that he had a Jewish grandmother. Suddenly Jewish blood had become a prime asset—apparently Jewish grandmothers abounded in German families. After he dropped his initial reserve he confided more of his worry about the future. He feared that the Americans would use the same methods against the Germans that the Nazis had used against us. When the American troops fired mortar shells at a snowy patch high up in the mountains he was rigid with fear that this spelled the beginning of a general retribution. He showed us a gun he had and asked what to do with it. We tried to reassure him, but to no avail. He threw all his weaponry down the slope into the woods below his home. Actually, the shooting, we learned later, was just a sort of target practice and amusement.

Karl and Greta, his wife, showed us our room with the four beds. The first thing I wanted to do was wash. Karl came up with jackets, pants, and underwear for all of us, and we found some that fit us well enough. There was a tragicomic aspect to our beginning to look like real people again so soon. I lay down on a bed with clean sheets and a down comforter, savoring every luxurious bit.

Next we sat down to a warm plate of soup, and stew with plenty of potatoes. We were about to explore the village and look for a barber when Karl told us that on a road behind his house the Germans had abandoned a truck. It was large and canvas-covered, and filled with what must surely have been headquarters supplies. Hundreds of boxes of fifty cigars, each covered in tin to keep it from drying out, were part of the cargo. There were numerous pairs of new, sturdy hiking boots, army raincoats, and countless cans of meat. We took as much as we could carry and stored our bounty in our room. Then we set out on a tour of the village. We must have been quite a sight, the four of us in our new boots and long German army raincoats. We could not find any open barbershop and were reluctant to force our way in as some other ex-prisoners and some American soldiers did. I felt drunk with the freedom to act and, above all, to live. What I wanted was to be human again more than to take revenge or savor my superiority over the Germans. My rage took a backseat. The fantasies of revenge that had filled our days were forgotten.

My thoughts again turned to Nora and other friends

and relatives. I wondered about Dorus, and whether Dachau was liberated. How long was the war going to last? There were rumors that Hitler was dead and that negotiations were under way. We listened eagerly to the radio. That evening a friend of Greta's stopped by at our hosts', bringing with her the two fellows who had escaped from the train near Scharnitz on the Austrian border. It was a strange evening. We had almost forgotten what it was like to sit down in a living room and have tea and cakes. There was talk about politics, worry about the Communists and the plundering, raping Russian troops. We were very thankful to be under American occupation forces. Finally I could no longer keep my eyes open and withdrew to my bed. Although I was not religious I felt compelled to offer thanks for having survived, for all the lucky breaks that had come my way, and to pray for Nora's survival as well, not to mention our anticipated reunion in Holland. I felt this very intensely, in contrast to my general lack of emotions, a lack the others experienced too.

I slept into the late morning. After breakfast in the kitchen, Karl, seeming quite anxious, joined us. He was afraid of being put out of his home by the American troops who had occupied the village and had already requisitioned some homes. He hoped that having us stay at his house would afford him some protection. He gave us some pocket money for haircuts and whatever else we might need. Perhaps not surprisingly, I found myself identifying with him and his worries about being evicted from his home. It revived recent painful memories. Yet I did not rejoice about the tables being turned; my overwhelming desire was for an end to all wars or warlike acts and for a secure, civilized life.

Reality intruded abruptly into my hazy, idealistic state of mind in the form of an army captain and his men. They liked the house, as we had when we chose it, and decided to make it their headquarters. Karl and his family would have to leave in a few hours, and we also, as civilians, were not allowed to stay under the same roof with them. But, after some discussion in which Ellis did most of the negotiating in very good English, we were allowed to stay overnight. The captain promised to have us and our belongings taken to a camp for displaced persons set up in the barracks of an elite German mountain corps on the north side of town. He thought that from there we would find transportation back to our home countries.

Ernst and Max decided to find some other place to stay and then return home in a few days. The war had apparently come to a halt. The Germans had surrendered. Berlin had been taken by the Russians, and Hitler was dead. I learned that on leaving Holland the Nazis had flooded parts of Zeeland and new polders in the Zuiderzee and destroyed most means of mass transportation. The result was chaos. Here and there we heard that it would be wiser not to rush back to Holland.

Having to evacuate our beautiful newfound home was hard to accept. It felt like a step backward, away from the world we had dreamed about and returned to. The Americans asked Ellis and me if we would help them to organize a clinic and emergency room in the camp for displaced persons. They would give us every possible assistance, including medications and equipment. We agreed to help get it started but insisted on leaving at the first opportunity for the west and Holland.

That same night, after Karl and his family had left, the Americans explored the house and came up from the cellar with all kinds of canned food and fine wines, including champagne. The dinner they served up turned into a drunken brawl. It was my first alcohol in at least three years. I could not enjoy it all that much, but we felt disappointed in Karl and Greta, who could have treated us to some of the wine and other delicacies they had hoarded in their cellar. I felt as if our little Shangri-la had been swallowed up again by the turmoil of the war and its aftermath. I retired quite early and again slept far into the next morning.

XXIV

We were moved to our new quarters by army trucks. The barracks were located in a picturesque section of the valley amid lush green meadows and babbling streams. As we came closer, we saw women walking in the fields and realized that it was a camp for both men and women.

Ellis and I found a small but pleasant room with two beds and stored all our belongings in it. The women we had seen lived on the same floor and were part of the administration and girlfriends of the Americans in charge. They originally came from France, had worked in Germany, and oddly enough did not want to return to France, at least not yet. They must have volunteered to go to Germany and now were afraid of how they would be received back home; anyone who had volunteered was very likely a collaborator.

We explored the rest of the camp and found two barracks overflowing with former prisoners, many in poor physical health. In front of another building were two large mounds of ammunition that somebody was shooting at, creating a fantastic fireworks display of exploding bullets and other small ammunition. In another barracks we found an elaborate display of mountain-climbing gear complete with photographs of how the various tools were used and all kinds of weapons. I felt I had entered a strange surrealistic world in a state of near chaos.

We found evidence of lice among the ex-prisoners. The risk of typhus being high, we ordered all the DDT we could get and organized a system whereby everybody had to pass through the shower area and be sprayed with DDT, which was supposedly harmless to humans. We also found a copper solution used by the Germans, which we knew from Dachau. To compare its effectiveness with DDT we put some lice in test tubes with the two solutions. To our surprise and that of the American doctors, we found that the German solution worked much faster and better. It killed the lice in about ten minutes, while in the tubes with DDT they were still moving around six hours later.

We drove with one of the army physicians to the South Bavarian regional headquarters of the American army in Garmisch-Partenkirchen to get more equipment. It was a beautiful ride, but it could not quite dispel the insidious sense of being back in a prison camp. There was even a guard at the entrance, and permission was needed to go into the village. Out of principle I never complied, and nobody really bothered me, but the existence of such a rule was disquieting. The little alarm clock I had saved from the lab was stolen. Once I went shopping, and when I bought a loaf of bread with the money Karl had given me, the shopkeeper—surprised to see me pay—told me that many ex-prisoners had demanded bread for nothing. I just shrugged my shoulders, but deeper down I thought "good for them."

After two weeks of this peculiar life halfway between prison camp and the free world we were informed of a transport to Mannheim the next day. There we could decide whether to go to France or to Holland.

The ride to Mannheim was long and exhausting. There were about twenty of us, displaced persons and ex-prisoners, in the back of a large truck. Again I felt as if we were being treated like cattle, but this time I was under no constraint. We all had gone voluntarily and did not care as long as we were on our way home. After many hours, toward evening we arrived in Ulm, which had been reduced to rubble. Many blocks had disappeared entirely, and debris lined the streets. We drove up a hill to a kind of fort or citadel, where we spent the night.

After an ample dinner, Ellis and I found a large mess room, where we bunked down on top of a table. At noon we boarded a truck for Mannheim, where four hours later we arrived in another camp for displaced persons. Almost immediately on our arrival we met a group of about ten other Dutchmen who were also trying to get back to Holland. One of them, Jaap, was a middle-aged man who, in spite of his exhaustion and disheveled appearance, looked distinguished and spoke with a sophistication which made me feel instantly that he was a person of some importance. We were fortunate to have him as our leader; otherwise we might easily have gotten lost in this camp with thousands of people wandering around. It spread over a large area on the outskirts of the city, with many houses, all of which were open. The beds were available to anyone in need of rest. Before we used these facilities we arranged for our departure from the railroad station and settled where and when to meet later that evening. I had about two hours to walk around, eat, and rest.

It was a dizzying experience, not only because of the crowded conditions, but because of the variety of people of all ages, nationalities, war experiences, religions, physical conditions, attire, and education. One aspect stood out: there were hardly any women. I saw several people from Auschwitz, but no sign of Nora. Somebody mentioned Ravensbrück, as Münch had done, as a camp where many women from Auschwitz had ended up, and said they had returned by different routes. I thought of my parents, but I did not see any older people, and again I realized that they could not have survived. I did not dwell long on thoughts about them. I still was not able to mourn. Rather, I was savoring the notion of returning home to people and a life familiar to me, to getting in touch with my family in the United States and Australia. Life was a very fast whirl of events, like a dream or three-ring circus.

At the appointed time we met with our all-Dutch group of about twenty-five and were bused to the railroad station. On the platform two trains stood ready, one for American troops, the other for ex-prisoners and displaced persons. The train for the Americans was a regular one with passenger cars; ours was made up of freight cars. Somehow we did not seem to mind. We divided our group into two smaller ones, one per car. This gave us plenty of room to lie down and make ourselves comfortable. Ellis managed to get a piece of real soap, scented at that, from the Americans in the other train. It evoked memories of old times far away and yet maybe quite close again. Jaap had decided that we could not go directly to Holland. The situation there was still too chaotic without any mass transportation, so we headed for Paris as an intermediate stop.

Around midnight we began our slow journey westward across the Rhine. There were frequent stops, usually between stations. The railroads still seemed to be working in a rather primitive fashion. Also, our train must have had a very low priority, and frequently it was shunted off the only available track. Later that morning we arrived in a town in eastern France, and from there we again were bused to another transit center near Saarbrücken.

There for the first time we passed through a real check; American army personnel took down our names and destinations. I tried to find out whether it was possible to send a message to my family in the United States. The Americans were not encouraging, but I still gave them an address in New York that I remembered.

After a wait of some hours Jaap announced that we could not proceed to Paris immediately but would be bused to a small camp in a little village in farming country between Châlons-sur-Marne and Verdun. On arrival we were taken to a large barn with two rows of cots. There, in the backyard of a farmhouse, we found two men and two women, also Dutch, lounging near a little stream. They behaved rather strangely. No word of welcome, but instead an inquiry about who we were and what we wanted.

We ignored them and decided to explore the village, Sermaize. We found out that there was another larger camp, Etrepy, nearby to which we were to move the next day. We retired early. Our four unfriendly compatriots did not bother to tell us that the water was contaminated, and as a result everybody developed serious intestinal problems later that night. It took me about a month and a half to recover.

The next day we moved into army tents in the larger camp. But before moving I went to the local post office and asked whether cables to New York were being accepted. They were, and I sent a brief message to the firm where my brother worked, telling him that I was in good health and on my way home. Once the cable was sent I confessed to the clerk that I had no money but that I did have cigars. He readily agreed to accept them in lieu of cash. After some bargaining we finally agreed on eighty cigars, an exorbitant amount by any standard but as far as I was concerned well worth it. However, I was foolish to trust him. I learned later that the cable was never sent. In this camp I again met Sam, a Dutch block-elder and ex-boxer I had known at Auschwitz. He had only recently recovered from typhus. I noticed, as with several others who recovered from typhus, that he had undergone a marked personality change; he had become very suspicious and quite hard of hearing.

It was the middle of May, and the weather was beautiful. Ellis and I took a much-needed, refreshing swim in a nearby river. The delay in getting to Paris began to bother us; after two days of waiting we thought about going on our own and trying to hitch a ride on military vehicles. But Jaap finally got our papers straightened out, and we left for Paris on a real passenger train. We traveled together with French prisoners of war and were greeted enthusiastically at stops along the way with flags, bands, and refreshments—a smaller but nonetheless welcome version of my fantasies about homecoming, even if we were merely hangers-on of the French prisoners of war.

In Paris, too, a big crowd and a lot of excitement awaited us. We were met by some members of a Dutch mission to the French government who assisted displaced persons in finding lodgings. We were taken to a room where, as had become the custom, we had to wait until they decided where to put us for the night. An hour and a half later we at last arrived in the large basement of a building that had been converted into a dormitory. Some other representatives of the Dutch government came to see us, one of them the chief medical officer. When he learned that Ellis and I were physicians he immediately offered us a paid job, room and board included, as his assistants. In view of the bad situation in Holland we decided to accept, especially since he told us that we could accompany weekly transports of patients being repatriated to Holland. This would give us a chance to decide for ourselves when we wanted to return to Holland.

The Dutch mission was on the boulevard Malesherbes, normally the office of the Dutch chamber of commerce. When we arrived there the next day we were given new clothes, shoes, and a room at a hotel where most of the people who worked at the mission were staying. I felt very excited. Suddenly I was self-supporting and had a place to live. Even more important, I met a certain Mr. van Dam, who had known my brother well before the war. He was most helpful in furnishing me with an affidavit to the Dutch consul so that I could get a new Dutch passport, and also in forwarding mail to my brother in the United States and my sister in Australia.

All this helped in my return to civilization. Yet to a certain extent things and people were not yet quite real. I still felt as though I were recuperating from a serious illness and had been given a moratorium with regard to assuming full responsibility for my new job. I felt that I was entitled to certain exceptions and privileges, a feeling that may well have been encouraged by many of the people I was involved with.

My job consisted chiefly of tending to the physical checkups of new arrivals or occasional emergencies, which we usually referred to local physicians or hospitals. Ellis returned to Holland with the first convoy two weeks after our arrival and decided to stay. I worked in Paris and some detention camps in the surrounding countryside. These brought back memories of the concentration camp, for I had to examine Dutch citizens who had been members of the S.S. I felt acutely uncomfortable in a role giving me a certain degree of authority over traitors. My memories were still much too fresh and the wounds too raw, and I asked to be relieved of this responsibility.

I spent much time wondering about Nora. Thinking about her made me somewhat aloof and unreceptive to the charms and flirtatious advances of the women at work. I was determined to wait for her and refused to entertain the possibility that our reunion might never come to pass.

On returning from a short trip in early June, I found a telegram from Nora's parents in Palestine. The telegram said that Nora had returned to Holland and was in Amsterdam. The repatriation bureau would know her address. I felt elated, told everybody in sight, and made preparations to go to Holland as soon as possible.

A few days later an opportunity opened up for me to accompany a group of fifteen seriously ill patients. We were to leave by plane on 6 June, my twenty-seventh birthday and the first anniversary of D day.

XXV

The plane was an air force DC–3. The weather was terrible, and we flew below the clouds. The turbulence made everybody sick except the crew. After what seemed an eternity but was actually only an hour and a half, we landed in Eindhoven, in the south of Holland, not far from where Nora and I had crossed the border during our escape attempt. The patients were immediately transferred to a hospital. A nurse and I got a ride to the main road to the north, where we had to try our luck hitchhiking on military vehicles, practically the only available means of transportation.

The nurse got a ride immediately. I stood alone on the road with most of my worldly possessions stuffed into a small bag, feeling neither loneliness nor sadness but, oddly enough, an unusual sense of power. I was about to reenter my country after a long, nightmarish absence. I felt older, possibly even wiser, and ready for whatever awaited me. Nothing could be worse than what I had experienced and witnessed over the past three years. And even though my feeling of euphoria did not last, a small nugget remained with me as a permanent protective shield. At the time I did not feel the pain of coming back to my ravaged and plundered homeland, with so many of my friends and family, my parents in particular, gone. I felt this day as a good birthday, even better than the previous one, which had coincided with D day. The sixth of June 1945 was my very own private D day, an anticipation of my reunion with Nora.

A truck stopped to give me a ride just as I was formulating these thoughts. We crossed the Maas and the Rhine, over makeshift Bailey bridges; the old ones had all been blown up. I took in the sight of the green meadows and flowering orchards, and the fresh fragrance of the spring air. Before I knew it we were in Utrecht. I remembered that my old friends Mick and Ed lived on the very street we were driving along, and on an impulse I asked the driver to stop at their home. The truck waited while I rang the doorbell. Mick opened the door. I signaled the truck to go on; when she saw me she almost fainted. She had believed me dead.

We embraced and climbed up the stairs to the apartment. Of course I had to stay the night and tell them everything. We talked and talked. It was both exhilarating and sad, because of all our missing and lost friends, yet wonderfully good to be back with my old friends in my university town in my country.

After dinner I went to see another friend, Guus, a physicist. He had lost his father early in the war and was still living in the same house with his mother. We boiled some water on a little wood stove in the kitchen for tea. There was no gas yet, and coal was very scarce. We caught up a little on our experiences. I learned that Anton was all right in Friesland, where he had been in hiding, and was planning to return in the summer. His parents were also safe in their home in Zaandam, and the rest of his family as well.

Early that evening I returned to Mick and Ed and their warm hospitality and fell asleep, exhausted, home at last. The next day I hitchhiked to Amsterdam. I arrived in the afternoon and found Jan, who before the war had taken over our uncle's law practice, in an old patrician house on the Keizersgracht, one of the main canals. He was wearing a Dutch army officer's uniform. His duties encompassed

the coordination of civilian legal matters, including the restoration of property stolen by the Nazis to their legitimate owners. He had been a close friend of my family and knew where things had been hidden. He actually still had some of my parents' jewelry in his safe. I learned that my parents had been transported to Sobibor in Poland, and there had been gassed. As before, I could not really let this sink in. My return and the rediscovery of close friends was so overwhelming that I pushed my parents' death into the background. It seemed I had no control over this act of omission.

Jan had a motorcycle and drove me to the repatriation center where Nora was staying, just around the corner from where my parents and I had lived till the very last. But I simply did not notice our house as we passed. Jan dropped me off at the building where Nora was supposed to be, and I went inside.

I learned that Nora was out and was not expected to return until evening. But I did find two friends of hers. Bep, a woman I had known in Auschwitz, had been in the same block as Nora. We had dinner and then went for a walk. Bep wanted to warn me of changes in Nora. She was very discreet in telling me about their experiences after leaving Auschwitz. Actually, very little that she told me stuck in my memory, except that immediately after their liberation Nora was involved with some man in Germany. So was Bep, and she stressed that this had not meant much to either of them. Yet it reminded me of the doorkeeper's accusations in Block 10, and again I became strongly apprehensive. They had thought and talked about me, Bep continued, but had not expected me to survive. She didn't elaborate, and I didn't probe. She also repeated that Nora had changed. She had become tougher and physically heavier. Cautiously, Bep painted a less than pretty picture.

I told her I didn't care, that Nora had had to protect herself, and that she would revert to her former self once we were reunited. I was still full of anticipation. In my travel bag I had a bottle of perfume I had bought for Nora in Paris. Yet as the reunion I had longed for so deeply drew closer I felt a growing unease. When Bep and I returned from our walk we found Nora in her room.

When she saw me she looked stunned, astonished that I had found her. We embraced and held each other for a long time. Tears welled up in my eyes, and when we let go of each other I saw that her eyes, too, were filled with tears.

I told her that I had received a cable from her parents in Paris, where I was working for the Dutch government. I didn't know how they had found out where I was. I told her of my doubts and worries that she might not have survived the march from Auschwitz, the endless train rides, the hunger and thirst, but that I had never really lost hope.

I kissed her once more and noticed that she was wearing Catholic religious medals on a thin chain around her neck. I asked her where she had gotten them, and she told me that they had been given to her by an ex-prisoner she had met after liberation. She said that although they'd had sexual relations it had not meant anything to her. I asked her to remove the medals, and she answered that she'd think about it. Changing the subject, she said that her parents were very lucky to have been part of an exchange of Jews against money and some Germans in 1944 and to have been sent to Palestine. She reminded me how we had dreamed about going to Palestine and working in a hospital.

As we continued our reminiscences she told me that she believed her brother Bob to be dead, that her brother Bernard and his girlfriend, Susan, had made it to Spain and Switzerland and were supposed to return soon. Joop had not come through the war alive. He had continued to work in the underground, had been caught twice, and had escaped both times. It seemed as though he had managed to outsmart the Nazis. But they caught him a third time, and he was killed trying to escape from the camp in Vucht.

I told Nora what a strange trick of fate it was that our

first meeting on Dutch soil should be only half a block from where Joop and I had made our escape plan. We had come full circle. I also spoke about my parents' death in Sobibor, and then steered the conversation to our future. I asked whether she would come to Paris with me. I was certain that I could get her a job as a nurse with the Dutch mission. I could see some of the old sparkle return to her eyes. She was eager to come.

A strict curfew and separation of the sexes were enforced at Nora's shelter. We kissed each other good night and went to our respective rooms. Once I was back in my bed and could relax a little I realized that I missed the closeness I had felt in Auschwitz when I talked with Nora under her window every morning before going off to the lab in Raisko. Seeing her and hearing her voice then had been a sacred source of power that gave me strength to go on, no matter what the odds. Now I missed that very special feeling of intimacy and love. I wondered why she had not gotten in touch with Anton's parents or other relatives as we had promised each other in Auschwitz. We had agreed to meet there in case we lost each other.

After lights out and a bed check I returned to Nora's dorm and spent most of the night with her. The bed was very small and we had no privacy, but we were together in each other's arms without fear of the crematorium.

My trip to The Hague the next morning was an emotionally jarring experience. I used my official position to obtain a train ticket. On the surface everything seemed to function reasonably well in the station, but once on the platform I realized that all the electric wiring was shot and that our train was made up of antique cars pulled by an even older steam locomotive riddled with bullet holes. We left on time and proceeded slowly toward Haarlem. There we stopped for repairs.

During the half-hour stop on that familiar platform, on which I and my family and friends had waited hundreds of times—it is the station used by the residents of Bloemendaal—I began to feel terribly sad and painfully moved. Suddenly it came to me that my parents and many of my friends were gone forever. The houses across the tracks—everything—seemed empty, abandoned, like a ghost town. There was none of the joyous welcome of my dreams. I felt painfully alone.

The train was starting up again; suddenly people were milling about, and the city of Haarlem came to life. Everyone seemed to me imbued with a pioneer spirit, looking forward to new adventures. The steam engine broke down three-quarters of the way to The Hague; apparently it had breathed its last. I was back to hitchhiking, and I got to The Hague in reasonably good time. The center of the city had suffered extensive bomb damage. The ruins were convincing evidence that there had indeed been a war, a holocaust, that everything had changed and would never be the same anymore.

I had a reunion with two cousins. One had managed to escape to Switzerland, but his father, my father's brother, his sister and her husband, and two children were all gone, deported. His mother survived in hiding. The other cousin, a girl, had been deported to Theresienstadt in Czechoslovakia but survived. Her parents, another brother of my father, his wife, and her sister, husband, and children had not been so lucky. It was impossible for me to comprehend this almost total destruction of whole families. All my experiences could not make it any more real.

XXVI

The next day Nora and I traveled to Haarlem to visit Henk, an old friend of the family, who had been our dentist. We had been informed that my parents had left a suitcase with clothes and other belongings with him. It was my first venture back into Bloemendaal, our home until that fateful day when we were exiled to the Amsterdam ghetto. I found our dentist friend and his wife little changed. He and his house were the same; but I wasn't. I felt an emptiness, a sense of incompleteness, a stranger in my own hometown.

Repossessing my clothes, among them an almost new suit, helped to restore a feeling of self and respectability, but that did not dispel my sense of being merely a temporary visitor, of not belonging, even though I knew that Henk and his wife had been active in the resistance and they had received us with the utmost warmth and hospitality. They asked us to stay the night, and we gladly accepted. After dinner, before nightfall, I could not resist the temptation to visit our old home; it still belonged to us. The people who had rented it still lived there, sharing it with a few other families. Seeing the house was both painful and salutary. It was still there and was ours again. We walked around the neighborhood, passing by the home of a family we had known well. Their daughter, Lies, who was my age and had gone to school with me, saw us and invited us in. In typical Dutch fashion, the whole family and friends were gathered in a large circle sipping tea, discussing the events of the day and catching up on their lives. A man in army uniform with the rank of colonel told us that he was to take a small diplomatic convoy to Paris the next day. What a stroke of luck! He invited us to join him early next morning at the military barracks in Haarlem and return to Paris with him. Lies told us how she had managed to survive the war working as a nurse. It was an unusual, exciting evening, in which I went back in time to school days, moved into my childhood environment briefly, and left again the next morning for Paris together with Nora. A strange and unsettling experience. This was a life of constant improvisation, without a script, plan, or structure.

We left as planned and had an uneventful drive to Brussels, where we stayed overnight. Nora had the address of Albert and Sonya, the doctor and his wife we had known in Mechelen and Auschwitz. They were staying in a small apartment in a building that housed other Auschwitz alumni. We met a few of them in the lobby; one of them, seeing Nora's religious medal, told her bluntly to take it off. She refused jokingly; he became angry, twisted the thing off the chain, and threw it away. It made me feel good—that amulet had been a thorn in my side. Perhaps I had been too patient, waiting for Nora to remove it herself. In retrospect, the amulet was an omen of things to come. I no longer felt that Nora was all mine.

Neither Nora nor I thought of Brussels as the place where we had been taken prisoner or as the site of St. Gilles, nor did we want to go and see what the prison looked like. These memories belonged to a different era from the present. I now wonder how much our relationship suffered from the almost impossible task of bridging these two disparate worlds. When we were taken to St. Gilles and later to Auschwitz we lost contact with the world we knew, and now that we were reentering that world we seemed conversely to have lost touch with the world of the Holocaust. Yet that horrible world held its grip on our love for each other as if our feeling of love could not be salvaged. Was this the price we had to pay for our return to civilization?

Early the next morning we rejoined our guide and continued toward France. Everything went smoothly until we reached the border. Even though Nora's name appeared on the official Dutch list of members of the group, the French border guards would not let her pass because she had no passport. Nothing we did or said could budge their officious stubbornness. It occurred to me that where reason failed cigars might do the trick. I had learned to appreciate the power of smokes—it was far greater than money and less obvious than a bribe. I placed a box of twenty-five cigars unobtrusively yet clearly in their field of vision and smell. Without any further ado they stamped some piece of paper and handed it to Nora, and off we went.

In Paris, Nora, as I had anticipated, was given a job as a nurse in the Dutch mission where I worked. We shared a room in the hotel I had stayed at before. It would have been the ideal setting for a honeymoon, everything I had dreamed and wished for. But it became obvious that something elusive, intangible, was missing. There was a certain blandness on her part, a hesitation on mine; we were somewhat blasé, like an old married couple. Moreover, Nora really had to have a passport, and she went back to Holland to get it. Shortly after her return to France she was assigned to a camp in an old castle southeast of Paris. I was stationed closer to Paris, and it was a long trip from her place to mine. When I visited her the first weekend after her return, I was surprised to find Manny, an old friend of hers, there as well. He had hitchhiked to Paris after Nora obtained her passport. I had met Manny during the war at the N.I.Z. Hospital in Amsterdam. He was a sort of guitar-playing writer-philosopher and artist. It was difficult to get angry at him or to feel jealous, but it was obvious that something was going on between the two. I was called back to my station by an emergency, so we had no time to talk matters over and clear up any possible misunderstandings.

In the United States, meanwhile, after many weeks of suspense, doubt, and persistent hope, Lex received a cable from Frans, who had met Nora and me on my visit to Amsterdam. Lex spoke of our return as "the first ray of sunshine in a dark night." I had not cabled him from Paris, assuming wrongly that the message I had sent from Sermaize and my letter mailed from Etrepy a couple of days later had reached him. We had stayed over at Sermaize and Etrepy on the way to Paris in the middle of May. So it was actually not until June that Lex and the rest of my family in America learned that Nora and I were alive. Lex immediately notified Nora's parents and everybody else concerned.

Nora's parents wrote to him:

The day that we received your heavenly telegram informing us of the safe return of Louis and Nora we entered a new phase in our life. We have already received four letters from Nora and they were so many rays of sunshine in our quiet and gray existence without our children. Nora writes with a joie de vivre *which is very contagious. It is a miracle after all they experienced. Also Louis's letters are evidence of an unbroken will and an equally courageous spirit. You know of course that they are now in France. We really think they are somewhat too energetic to start work so soon. Half a year of rest would not have been a luxury. Why don't they go to townhall or a rabbi and get married? The last remnant of our bourgeois mentality which we all lost in the camps, but yet . . . ! Louis wrote in his letter, "You must come soon to Holland; then we will celebrate our wedding." It is, however, impossible to travel as yet; that will take us still quite a while. They should not wait for that. Your father frequently said, when he sat down with us in our little room in Westerbork, "The first thing we do when these* rotmoffen *[rotten Nazis] are gone, is celebrate Nora's and Louis's wedding." We then still had the childish optimism that we would eventually return straight from Westerbork to our homes.*

Now Louis and Nora have returned and are so intensely rejoicing in their freedom and the beautiful things in life for which they literally fought with their youthful will-power. Now they can really claim victory, having escaped this indescribable whirlpool of misery and crime. We are in heaven and everybody is rejoicing with us.

About a week later, Nora wrote me a brief note explaining that she was in turmoil and no longer sure of her feelings for me. She suggested that we talk about our future and make sure that if we parted we would do so in the same warm and tender spirit that had marked our past. Thus my suspicions were confirmed, much to my regret and deepest anguish.

We did meet several days later at the camp where I was working at the time, a converted country estate south of Paris. Nora looked a little like her old self, quite attractive in her army uniform, as we sat down on the veranda of the white main building looking out over a lawn bordered by big old trees. The only sounds to be heard were bird calls, and in the distance a door closing.

Nora started very directly, saying that we had changed, maybe while still in Auschwitz or maybe afterward, but that she felt different and believed that I did too.

I agreed, but said I was not yet ready to give up on us. She felt that perhaps I no longer found her as attractive as before. I admitted that there was some truth to that, but putting it in these terms was an oversimplification. I didn't really understand what had happened; she had meant everything to me, and without her I would not be sitting there now. Nora said that she possibly did not need me as much as I had needed her, that she was unsure of our relationship. I told her that I was afraid of letting her go, of being alone; yet despite my fear I also knew that this was not a good enough reason to hold onto each other. At this point Nora took my hand, and we looked at each other with tear-filled eyes and kissed and embraced wordlessly. We knew we were parting.

I was the first to break the silence by commenting on the incongruity of our situation. After all, there was no doubt in my mind that we could have a good life together—though perhaps we, or at least I, had taken it too much for granted. Perhaps I had never really made a conscious decision to get married, for during the war it was almost irrelevant whether we actually were married. But the situation had changed. Marriage represented a very important step, and neither of us seemed quite ready for it.

Nora agreed. Lost in thought, and rather sadly, she admitted that she had changed, that she seemed to have become more casual and superficial or perhaps adventurous. She felt it would be a mistake for her to make a commitment for the rest of her life, that the world, and she in particular, was in turmoil. And so we ought to part now, while we still treasured our relationship and still brought to it the warmth and respect that had marked it from the outset. We sat silently for a while, then got up and walked to the station once again.

The news of our separation came as a shock to our family and friends. We each wrote them about it without much of an explanation other than that we had changed. Nora's father wrote to Lex on 3 November 1945:

For several months now our contact has been interrupted by the lightning bolt of Louis's and Nora's separation. It produced a short circuit which to our great sadness broke off the ties which had linked us so sensitively. We believe after all that Nora and also Louis wrote us that their decision to part ways was prompted by pure motives from the deep wells of their soul. Therefore it might be called a sensible decision. Differing considerations and wishes from others, after all, have to remain silent.

To me our separation was another heavy loss against which I protected myself with the tools I had acquired in the Holocaust. I had to accept the reality of it. I reached out for old and new friends and my remaining family. I began to plan on completing my medical studies and combining my specialization in neurology and perhaps psychiatry with life near my family in America. My heightened sense of freedom and appreciation of life in general combined with an intense hunger to savor it fully helped to overcome the painful wound.

XXVII

The delay of almost forty years in writing this account of my war experience has prompted from myself and others many questions that I have found difficult to answer. After much thought, I have come to the conclusion that the term *Geheimnisträger* (bearer of the secret) contains a clue to understanding the long interval. This word had a very specific meaning in the camp. It denoted certain inmates who knew too much and hence were eliminated on short notice, usually in the gas chamber. To a certain extent every inmate, as soon as he knew of the genocide, experiments with human beings, and other such crimes, became a Geheimnisträger. Such prisoners were not supposed to survive lest they give testimony to these hellish crimes. Strangely, the sense of being a Geheimnisträger, of having been a witness to or merely of having known of such unimaginable horrors, did not disappear after the war but lingered on. This notion was something to be erased as soon as possible. Apparently it affected some who were not inmates of the camps, including people in top Allied government positions. It was as if one were forbidden to bear witness on penalty of death.

The S.S. and other perpetrators of these crimes, which they justified as necessary for the protection of their pristine racial and political character (Lifton 1986), made enormous efforts to keep their actions hidden from the world. The Final Solution was top secret, and the death camps were enveloped by an effective veil of secrecy. Some camps were even designated *Nacht und Nebel* (night and fog), invisible to the rest of mankind. It was not unlike the secrecy that surrounds weapons of the most awesome, destructive power. The isolation of Auschwitz consisted not only in its remote geographical location but also in the silence of the few neighboring villagers who could see the flames or smell the stench. Some of them even worked with inmates. This same wall of silence was encountered by three inmates who, in an unusual and rare successful escape to Czechoslovakia, ran into unexpected problems when they tried to break through this wall, to communicate. Their detailed account, scrupulously verified, was shelved when it eventually reached London and Washington (Kulka 1975).

The only blatant break in the wall of secrecy occurred when the camp was bombed erratically in August 1944, while I was recovering from my appendectomy. Many inmates, including myself, believed at first that it was the Nazi air force who dropped the bombs and that the Nazis blamed the Allied air force as a ruse to cover their tracks. I could not believe that the Americans or British would do anything so callous. Actually, the Allies had three bombs left after a raid on the I.G. Farben Buna complex and wanted to get rid of them before the long flight back. It was also difficult to believe that any Allied soldier had really seen Auschwitz. Encouraging as such a direct contact might have been, I do not remember anyone who felt it was worth the price of all the lives lost.

Memory for such terrifying events can indeed be tricky. I observed distortions of actual feelings in a relatively recent interview with a survivor of that bombing. He remembered the bombing as some sort of blessing. He did not seem to mind the serious injury or his close call—he almost lost his life because there was a selection in the course of his recuperation. He appeared to have forgotten his fear and agony. Our memories of the event were diametrically opposite. I remember the group of wounded inmates to which he belonged, on the same floor of the camp hospital where I was recuperating. They were terrified of the selections, wanting to live more than ever. The person whom I interviewed, knowing a selection was coming, had managed to get out of the hospital just in time. He and one other inmate were the only ones of the group wounded in this bombing to survive.

Since the war's end, especially in the past ten years, there has been considerable discussion of the failure of the Allied forces to bomb the camps. Apparently this move was considered but never adopted as a strategic goal. In *No Haven for the Oppressed* Saul S. Friedman writes that Chaim Weizmann suggested early in 1944 to the Allied high command that they bomb the railway lines to the camps and crematoriums. Friedman mentioned the risk to the lives of the inmates, but he qualifies this consideration with the comment: "It is doubtful that the prisoners would have cared, for they were doomed already. There might have been satisfaction, however, in knowing that through one's death the camps would cease to function." In view of my own experience during the random bombing of Auschwitz, I must say that I consider it fortunate that the Allied high command did decide not to bomb the camps "systematically." Railroad tracks can be repaired in a matter of hours, and the Nazis knew how to kill people in unbelievable numbers even before the existence of gas chambers and crematoriums, as Babi Yar demonstrated.

Apparently it is impossible for anyone who was not part of this camp world to sense or grasp fully the urge to live of those who ultimately survived. I believe a far more effective approach would have been to publicize the extermination process through all the media available at that time, and to include the names of the perpetrators known in Washington and London—in brief, to have let it be known that the secret was out.

I experienced a similar isolation or shelving after my liberation, if not in the course of my imprisonment. I wanted to return to "normal" civilized life as soon as possible and tried to shed my memories of that other sinister world. I even tried with some success to erase the number tattooed on my forearm. I wanted to rid myself of this tangible souvenir of the whole experience. Initially, I was quite successful in avoiding any reference to this period. Friends and family readily complied with this censure. There was what could be called a conspiracy of silence. Unlike some of my Auschwitz friends, I did not have any dreams, as far as I remember, about the camps. It was not until several years later, when I began my own analysis while a psychiatric resident, that I began to dream about being lost in strange lands, being separated from those closest to me, including my parents, and being back in a camp trying to escape. Invariably I would wake up before I made it to freedom. It was not until many years later that such dreams receded, but they did not disappear completely. The conspiracy of silence persisted in an emotional sense in my personal analysis. I would talk about my war experiences, but emotionally these were left largely untouched.

In writing this book at first I found my memory of the Holocaust unusually intact. It felt as if I were right back—indeed, vividly reliving the past. But when I had the opportunity, after all these years, of having Nora read an early draft of the manuscript, it became clear that both of us had forgotten segments of our joint experiences. She had forgotten parts that I remembered and vice versa. One situation that I had blotted out and only gradually remembered as a true experience was a regular event in the camp in Mechelen. The humiliating and frightening character of the experience, which incorporated some of the essence of concentration camp life, explains some of this forgetting. The S.S. commandant had the perverse habit of requiring that every prisoner stick his bare feet out from under the blanket so that the commandant could inspect them for any speck of dirt. For this purpose he would make rounds of the dormitories after bedtime. Any prisoner who failed this test had to go outside barefoot and partly dressed to do "sport" in the snow or mud. Pneumonia was a common sequel. Fortunately, it never happened to me. There being no water in the dormitory, we would use spittle to clean our feet. It took me about a week to remember this fully, to know it was my own experience and not something I had been told forty years after the fact. This was to me a powerful demonstration of how memory for such catastrophic times can be disturbed in unusual ways.

I had a habit that may be related to this type of forgetting. I would regard my mind as an absolutely private domain, where I could think defiantly or imagine anything without concern or fear of the S.S. authority who controlled my outside life. During the long, tedious hours of standing at *Appell* (roll call), while the S.S. guards would count their treasure of prisoner-slaves, I would envision the guard who might be standing right in front of me being killed in the worst possible manner. Perhaps this fantasy life facilitated the creation of a secret depository or cluster of memories that could be "lost" after the war. Yet during the war and life in the camp it was essential to have a few close and trusted friends with whom to share such secrets. On my way to and from the laboratory I had the opportunity to share confidences with some of my colleagues, especially confidences about people like Zabel, who to us were the incarnation of everything evil. Of course with Nora I could share any secrets. Verbalizing such fantasies, as in analysis, helped to maintain a safe distance from the whole experience of Auschwitz life. It helped a little to bridge the unfathomable gap between Auschwitz and the civilized world. My friends and these talks made certain that we would not lose touch with civilization.

Grubrich-Simitis (1981) offers a more explicitly theoretical formulation of this balancing act: "In this connection the defense mechanism of denial, albeit of a particular quality, was of paramount importance. It proved most effective for survival in those prisoners who were able to combine this psychic 'closing off' of an unbearable external reality with an intense remembering of an idealized past and magical fantasizing of a better alternative world—all this without becoming psychotic, in spite of the apparent similarity with the psychotic withdrawal from object representations and the erection of an alternative, hallucinatory, restitutive world." The bonding process, described earlier, helped preserve a healthy amount of secondary-process thinking as a check on primary-process incursions. This is illustrated by the incident during the evacuation march from Auschwitz, when the sight of my gloves made by Nora put a stop to my sleepy, dreamy state of mind. The gloves represented her and the meaning of our relationship as very real in contrast with the intruding fantasies or mirages. As a result I woke up immediately.

The function of memory has been of central significance in psychoanalysis. In the early years patients were thought to be suffering from memories. Freud (1914) described the change in emphasis to working through and the connection between not remembering and repeating. The repetition, he said, would in disguise represent the "forgotten" memory and take the form of acting out, either outside the analytic situation or within it, in the transference relationship. In 1937 he returned to a discussion of remembering in the sense of limitations on this function when there is no active conflict in the transference that could give access to the past. Such limitations are not uncommon among Holocaust survivors. One might wonder whether this represents a condition where exploration of the past, undoing of resistance, should be handled more slowly and carefully than usually. Solnit (1984) suggests a balance between too little and too much memory. In dealing with trauma in children, he says, there should be a "trade-off between neurotic, not too costly distortions in exchange for achieving a sense of coherency about one's life and self." One could apply this suggestion to some survivors of the Holocaust. Nora once said, long after the war, with intense feelings of despair, "It becomes a bottomless pool of mud, which cannot be cleared."

It struck me how rarely my parents or references to their loss were in my conscious thoughts or dreams. That loss has been most difficult to work through. The intensity of my fear of losing them when I was helplessly listening at the top of the stairs, expecting them to be taken away any moment, is a sample of the emotions that I had locked away. It was mostly those feelings that made me decide I had to escape in spite of all the risks. One aspect of "closing off" this loss after the war was my preoccupation with the older doctor and his family who were deported from Mechelen instead of Nora and me. The ensuing three months' moratorium on our deportation was in retrospect lifesaving. I apparently felt worse about this than about having left my parents. The death of the doctor and his family became a screen for the loss of my parents. It helped to contain much of my anger and could explain some of my very civilized behavior toward the people in Mittenwald, such as paying for my bread rather than taking it, which was the common practice.

The absence and return of my interest in music, specifically the cello, touched on my efforts to deal with the loss of my parents. During the war, in 1940, stimulated by Nora's involvement in music, I began to play the cello again after at least ten years of not even touching the instrument. In contrast with my attitude in childhood and adolescence, I enjoyed playing it as an adult and in spite of the expense bought a new cello. My parents took obvious pleasure in my reinvestment in music. After the war, I found this cello where Anton had stored it safely for me, but I did not take up the instrument again. After my move to the United States, I left it in its black wooden case, which was very suggestive of a casket. I completely forgot about its being in my home. I left it in the attic, wholly unconcerned about what could happen to it in the heat or cold or humidity of that climatically uncontrolled place.

When, a while after the birth of my daughter, I looked in the cello case I was horrorstruck by the condition of the instrument. It was a terrible mess. The front leaf had sprung several cracks, some of the edges had become unglued, the soundpost was loose, strings were broken, and the bridge had fallen off. It was indeed like a disintegrating body. I brought it to a good repairman, and to my amazement he was able to restore it to its original state or even better. I could not get enough time practicing and playing it with friends.

Around that time, string instruments turned up in a dream in connection with one of the most respected and feared teachers of my residency and later my psychoanalytic training. The dream ran as follows: I was sitting in the back of the classroom—as if I were back in the Gymnasium in Haarlem—and the teacher was in front, facing the class, showing us an ancient violin. He asked us to name the period and origin of the fiddle. There were other fiddles hanging on the wall, as in a collector's home or museum. Nobody answered—I was hiding behind the others—but to my surprise and dismay I was attached to this fiddle with a long string, like a fishing line. He pulled me to the front, where I stood mortified, not knowing how to answer him; then I woke up. The teacher was a composite of teachers at all levels of my education, my father, myself, and Weber, the chief of the laboratory in Auschwitz. With a sadistic grin, Weber could ask the most impossible questions. The string instrument had to do with life. It was an inanimate object that could be brought to life with a beautiful tone, full of warmth and human emotion. It reminded me of a male nurse in the hospital in Auschwitz who would play the violin in the evenings when I was recuperating from diphtheria. My cello represented all this in kaleidoscopic fashion—

an awakening or rebirth after a long sleep, an attempt to put my past in a harmonious perspective with the present.

In order to explore the nature of a close relationship in the camp in more detail I must consider my relationship with Nora—which was after all the most crucial one of these friendships.

Our relationship had become more serious precisely at the time Holland surrendered to the Nazis. This cast a spell on it, a certain ambiguity. Questions, readily dismissed, would occur to me, like: Would I have returned with my parents to IJmuiden early on the day after the surrender if Nora and her parents had not joined us? My parents and I might have escaped. I imagined that such thoughts played a role in my mother's criticism of Nora. She had warned me that Nora tended to be careless about rules and might draw herself and me into difficulties with the Nazis. After my imprisonment in St. Gilles there were moments when I blamed Nora for getting me into this mess, but then I blamed myself for making the decision to escape or decided it was silly to blame anyone other than the Nazis. Most of the time I felt good for at least having tried to get out of the enemy's reach. Prison at that time was an honorable place. Any differences Nora and I had had appeared short-lived. In the face of the ever more threatening enemy they disappeared altogether. There was, however, one exception. Once, shortly after our move to Amsterdam, I had complained to Nora about her day-to-day approach to life, comparing it to my greater emphasis on the future. I was more willing to accept restrictions in the present in anticipation of making up for them later, maybe after the war. Although they were not discussed explicitly, there were probably some sexual frustrations due to naïveté and fear of pregnancy or neurotic anxieties. The ever-increasing threat to our very lives made it easier to overlook such issues than to work on them. For instance, the first mass deportation of four hundred young Jews in February 1941 and their reported death a short while after had made any of our difficulties look ridiculous.

Events in my early childhood may also be helpful in clearing up developments in my involvement with Nora. Separation had been quite painful for me even as a very young child. The first such event I can remember occurred when I was three years old. Our nursemaid, or "Juf," left. A discussion between mother and Juf took place during lunch one day, when I was the only other person present. (My brother and sister were probably in school.) Juf became very upset, tears running down her cheeks, and I very compassionately tried to console her. Many years later I learned that my mother, concerned that Juf had become too attached to me, had fired her that day. I remember my mother's fainting a few days earlier. She was lying on the bathroom floor, softly groaning, her eyes closed. I thought she was going to die or was dead, and I was terrified. Somebody was sponging her face with cold water. She came to and went to bed. This happened after a summer outing to the beach. Apparently there had been an argument between mother and Juf during the outing.

The following winter another experience left an indelible mark in my memory. During a walk with our new "Juf" I saw that a white horse pulling a delivery cart had fallen on the ice, could not get up, and was lying motionless on the road. Again I assumed the horse was dead, and I was frightened accordingly. Another "contact" with death occurred in those days in the shape of a Punch and Judy show. My father would give a performance with the puppets as a special treat on various occasions. One of the characters was Death, a white puppet with a head in the shape of a skull, the eye sockets and mouth painted black. I would run out of the room when he made his appearance. It was ironic that such a skull should appear again on the cap of the S.S. in Auschwitz. During the same winter—I was still three years old—my mother went to Berlin for a two-week visit to an uncle and aunt. I had been told about the trip a month in advance and imagined it would be a very long journey. I would get mixed up about time and ask my mother why she had not left yet or think the trip was canceled. When she actually left I was apprehensive, but my father was very good to us. He would often play with us and promised that mother would bring back a real steam engine, cars, and track. We sent her letters with drawings of the engine with lots of wheels. After her return with the precious engine everything seemed fine, but I did not get along very well with the new Juf and would cry a lot when my parents went out in the evening. I would wake at night and if they were not yet home stay awake until I heard them arrive back home safely.

This problem became rather an obsession when I was six years old. My parents, probably out of desperation, resorted to a trick, which if anything added insult to injury. In elementary school it was customary to celebrate St. Nicholas' birthday on 5 December. Saint Nicholas was three hundred years old, a bishop from Spain, dating back to the eighty-year war between Holland and Spain. He would arrive at the school, dressed in a gold-decorated miter and tabbard and seated in an open carriage drawn by two horses. His servant, Black Pieter, would carry two burlap sacks, one filled with presents and the other empty, to collect naughty children to be taken back to Spain. After a welcome from the principal, St. Nicholas would sit down on a throne on a platform in the gym. There in front of the gathered students and teachers he would open his large book in which everything about everybody was recorded. I was literally called on the carpet, scared to death but outwardly calm. Saint Nicholas would say: "Louis, you have been a very good student, your work has been excellent, but I noticed that you cry a lot when your parents are away from home; a boy your age should not mind that so much. Since you have been good otherwise here is a present for you." Of course I was greatly relieved that I was not carted off, "deported," to Spain.

In a belated insight it dawned on me, long after the war, that Nora had some features that for me were reminiscent of the first "Juf" and represented a motherly, nurturing aspect of Nora for me. Such Oedipal attributes were greatly enhanced, of course, by the unique situation in Auschwitz. When I was in the hospital with diphtheria, starving without even an indication of a way out of my predicament, her sudden reappearance at first in the form of nurture—a sandwich with a note that she was all right and within reach—could not have been more evocative of such Oedipal wishes and fantasies. My confinement to half a mattress gave me ample time for such fantasies in various disguises. Thus Nora became the ideal woman, who in reality was sexually out of reach. This fact further enhanced the fairytale nature of the relationship. When Derek, the block elder's helper and messenger between Nora and me, teased and challenged me, insisting that he could easily seduce Nora because "all those nurses in Block 10 are so hungry for sex," I argued with him. I told him with absolute conviction that Nora would be faithful to me under any circumstances. There was not the slightest doubt in my mind. It was the only way I could experience our relationship. The alternative would have literally killed me.

The way I would sneak up to her window to talk with her briefly before marching off to work had this very quality of fantasy. My sudden overwhelming distress when I was not allowed in her barrack by the "friendly" Münch was akin to the feelings of a little boy prevented from seeing his mother. There is other evidence that this magic quality remained an important part of my relationship with her throughout our stay in Auschwitz. It provided me with a sense of protection or immunity that sustained me through many harrowing experiences. Nora had always expressed an unwavering belief that we would survive—even at the moment we were trapped in the Brussels Gestapo office. The sudden blow of betrayal, loss of freedom, and anticipation of death had caused me to waver agonizingly between a

191

feeling of total devastation and a belief that it was just part of an arrangement with the underground to obtain the necessary documents. At least temporarily, she helped me to accept defeat and the notion that in the end we still might win.

At this point it is no longer so surprising that the relationship came to an end shortly after we met again at the close of the war. The early childhood elements interwoven with the effects of the camp situation had promoted a relationship that was ill suited for the postwar world. There were other reasons as well. Nora had changed physically and was in what she herself called, many years later, a "wild state of mind." After the bombing of Auschwitz in late summer 1944, her situation had gradually deteriorated; for a while she was made to do impossibly heavy labor. She was rescued from this life-threatening work by Vladimir Hanak, the physical education professor, who was able to get her lighter, indoor work. Thus she lived through the evacuation to Ravensbrück, where she was liberated.

There was at least one other reason that contributed to our going our separate ways. It was her explanation for the affair with another man: namely, that she had not expected me to survive, in such stark contrast to her conviction while we were in the camps. When others had expressed surprise at my survival, it was a reflection of general, not personal, relevance. I would take it as a sign of admiration, but when this came from Nora, as strictly personal, I felt as if it was a vote of no-confidence. Her continuing to wear the religious medal was a token to me of her disbelief or reluctance to accept the fact that I really had made it back. In spite of my attempt to deny her loss of faith this was too obviously a blow to my ego.

Let me here attempt to think aloud about the meaning of being a survivor. One reason I was so hurt by Nora's surprise about my return fully alive was that I felt it took some unusual fortitude to accomplish this and that she had surmised I did not possess this special ingredient. I am rather certain that I had my own doubts about this, so that she touched on a very sensitive area. I did not really feel like a survivor in the heroic sense. But to have been challenged by the "woman of my dreams" was very difficult to deal with. Although I survived in Auschwitz for two years I do not feel that I am what people usually have in mind when they talk about survivors. Even though I had my share of living in the shadow of death, the everyday situation for considerable periods of time could have been much worse. In contrast with Birkenau, the camp and barracks were relatively clean, free of mud, with regular toilets, running water, and no stench. Nourishment was inadequate, but there were enough extra supplies to sustain me. There were actually times without acute stress when I found myself musing that—compared with conditions in other camps, parts of the camp I was in, occupied countries, or the front—my life was not so impossible. I would end this thinking by berating myself for having such stupid thoughts. Indeed, one did not know what might happen the next day or hour, but it felt good to pretend that one could sit out the war in such paradoxical "comfort." There was certainly nothing heroic required of me the year I worked in the Raisko laboratory. There was a certain feeling of belonging to a coherent group of around fifty people who if necessary would help each other.

On the other hand, should one not also refer as survivors to those people who survived under the worst conditions in 1942—I knew some of these old-timers—and lived for three more years but were killed at the very end of the war in 1945? It appears to me that these people had the essential ingredient, or a will to sustain life without which survival was impossible. One definition of survivor coincides most closely with my own experience: someone who endures or lives in spite of wholly unfavorable odds to outlast his enemies. It concurs with the idea that to emerge alive from the Holocaust constituted a victory over Nazi ideology and its Final Solution. A proverb I learned in Holland conveys a similar meaning: "He who laughs last, laughs best." Hitler actually may have had this proverb in mind when he ranted in a nationwide speech in September 1942: "At one time, the Jews of Germany laughed about my prophecies. I do not know whether they are still laughing or whether they have already lost all desire to laugh. But right now I can only repeat: they will stop laughing everywhere, and I shall be right also in that prophecy" (Wyman 1984, 53).

Among those who have written on the subject of survival there is considerable diversity. Viewpoints range from a sense that it was all a matter of luck (de Wind 1981) to a sense that a "talent for life" and "*human* kinds of behavior, which cannot be reduced to a bit of datum in theory," were essential to survival (Des Pres 1976). Besides the unpredictable vagaries of fate, Des Pres wrote: "There must also be a move beyond despair and self-pity to that fierce determination which survivors call up in themselves. To come through; to keep a living soul in a living body." With all possible lucky breaks it was still essential to have this deep-felt need to live. To stay alive was to claim victory over tormentors, who would warn you over and over again not to have any illusions of surviving. Every Allied victory making the outcome of the war in our favor ever more obvious was a powerful force stirring our will to return alive. The intensity and the reality of this will—even in primary-process form—became manifest to me during my awakening from the anesthesia after my appendectomy. Fighting my imagined six S.S. guards with what felt like unbelievable power—I broke several leather belts—reflected this need to win. The same drive was apparent in a more constructive way during my three-week battle with peritonitis. These experiences coincided with the liberation of France, Belgium, and part of Holland and the expectation that Germany would collapse in a matter of weeks. I experienced a similar thrust of optimism on the two occasions when I received food parcels from Holland. They nurtured my bond with the other, old world. In Dachau my reunion with a number of old friends from my university, my alma mater, had a similar effect. To be able to imagine surviving helped me maintain a level of alertness and anticipation to outwit any schemes the S.S. and their collaborators would invent.

Fortunately, their repertory of tricks was limited. After a while one began to recognize certain basic rules. One was never to trust a promise made by any member of the S.S.—for example, "Arbeit macht frei." Second, it was most dangerous to know anything. A third rule, less well known, was that those inmates who flagrantly misused the power of their position in the inmate hierarchy eventually would lose control and fall by the wayside. In unexpected ways there were some checks and balances, a daily life of sorts. While in the camp I gained a tremendous respect for what a human being could tolerate on a routine basis.

When the smoke of the struggle for survival lifted after our liberation, Nora and I were left with serious doubt about the viability of our relationship. Although I did not realize it at the time, I am convinced that another important factor contributing to our parting grew out of my desire to forget the immediate past. It seems ironic that, after the war, living together would have reminded us, if only because of our special closeness, of that incomprehensible and threatening period in our lives. This was exactly the opposite of what happened in Auschwitz, where we represented to each other an essential link with the civilized world, which was otherwise out of reach. From my present vantage point, I assume that we both would have experienced a need to refer to our camp experiences whenever such memories were stirred up. Our living together would inevitably have increased the chance of this happening, no matter how deeply repressed, isolated, or walled off that period remained. Our wounds were still too raw to be touched. They had to be covered up to allow healing to take place.

It would be of great interest to explore in detail in terms

of psychoanalytic theory how this healing process takes place. But that would require a study by itself. In general it took the world about thirty years before it was ready to investigate this terrible chapter in the history of mankind. Anyone who has attempted to analyze survivors within five to ten years after the end of the war must have encountered an almost impenetrable wall of resistance if those persons were healthy enough and had the capacity to erect it. In terms of indications for analysis one could infer that in cases where one is dealing with intense and relatively recent trauma, analysis should be deferred or modified until after some basic healing has occurred. Be this as it may, in my own analysis in 1952 my Holocaust experience was beyond the grasp of my analyst and certainly myself. Fortunately, he seemed to recognize this and did not promote any exploration of these experiences in depth. I admired his patience. At the time of my second, training, analysis the wall had become less rigid. Gradually I have begun to view such resistance, in general, as not necessarily a neurotic feature but rather as a mode of defense against realistic pain, which has not yet moderated enough to allow analysis to proceed technically along the classical route.

Following this line of thought, it is obvious, at least to me, that Nora and I would have felt frustrated by each other's aloofness and inclined to attack the other's defenses. This would have initiated a vicious cycle of prolonged suffering and misery. Thus it becomes clear that our separation, surprising and contrary to so-called common sense, was a most fortunate decision. Perhaps intuitively respecting each other's needs to find a new path toward our individual goals within the renewed, invigorated dimension of a real future, we could separate harmoniously and maturely.

Before I conclude this tale, I want to follow up on Dorus, whom I last mentioned being put to bed in the Krankenbau in Dachau after he had ingested ten sleeping tablets. The trick worked perfectly, as he told me in the fall of 1945 during a visit to my room in Utrecht. He looked different, as did I, each of us with a full head of hair. Growing our hair certainly was the easiest part of our readjustment to civilized life. He described to me the fantastic spectacle of the liberation of Dachau. He was awakened by the sound of shooting after about twenty-four hours of deep sleep. The shooting constituted the first phase of the American ground troops' attack on the barbed-wire fence. The exchange of fire took place between the troops and the guards who were locked up in their towers. The second phase began when, heedless of the danger from the shooting in progress, hundreds of prisoners stormed the fence from within. They were waving American and other national flags which, incredible as it may seem, had been held in readiness for this occasion. The great photographer Margaret Bourke-White allegedly was one of the first to enter the camp, on a motorcycle. The S.S. men were rounded up and shot. Kees and Wim, the friends in the S.S. stockade, were saved from that fate by Tom at the last possible moment. The Americans of course assumed that they were S.S. men, as I had when I had first seen them.

Dorus had returned to his former job as a chemical engineer. My Dutch friends in Dachau, such as Tom, Wim, and Kees, also returned to Utrecht. Anton was back at his studies, but a large number of students, both Jewish and non-Jewish, did not return. Some tragically lost their lives during the very last days of the war.

Later I learned that Wirths, the chief S.S. physician in Auschwitz, had committed suicide by hanging. In September 1945 he reported himself to the British authority in the Northwest of Germany. After the initial interrogation the British officer shook hands with him and said: "Now I have touched the hand of somebody who murdered four million people. Think about this tonight, and I will see you in the morning." That night Wirths killed himself. Weber had been arrested but died of a kidney ailment. Münch was also arrested and was the only one of forty S.S. arraigned before a Polish tribunal who was acquitted, thanks to the testimony of former prisoners whom he had befriended. He returned to his practice in Bavaria.

Although I was long reluctant to begin writing this story, I now find it very difficult to put the whole matter to rest. But enough is enough, even if the ending seems arbitrary. The best I can do is to delegate this period in my life to the background, as it were, on my bookshelf, where I can pick it up whenever the present rather than past requires it.

BIBLIOGRAPHY

Des Pres, Terrence. 1976. *The Survivor: An Anatomy of Life in the Death Camps.* New York: Oxford University Press.

De Wind. 1981. Editorial in *Nieuwe Rotterdamse Courant Handelsblad,* February 14.

Freud, Sigmund. 1914. *Remembering, Repeating and Working-Through: Further Recommendations on the Technique of Psychoanalysis II,* standard edition. London: The Hogarth Press.

Freud, Sigmund. 1937. *Analysis Terminable and Interminable,* standard edition. London: The Hogarth Press.

Friedman, Saul S. 1973. *No Haven for the Oppressed: United States Policy toward Jewish Refugees, 1938–1945.* Detroit: Wayne State University Press.

Grubrich-Simitis, Ilse. 1981. "Extreme Traumatization as Cumulative Trauma: Psychoanalytic Investigations of the Effects of Concentration Camp Experiences on Survivors and Their Children." In *Psychoanalytic Study of the Child,* vol. 36, ed. Albert J. Solnit, Ruth S. Eissler, Anna Freud, Marianne Kris, and Peter B. Neubauer, 415–51. New Haven: Yale University Press.

Kulka, Erich. 1975. "Five Escapes from Auschwitz." In *They Fought Back,* ed. and trans. Yuri Suhl. New York: Schocken.

Lifton, Robert Jay. 1986. *The Nazi Doctors: Medical Killing and the Psychology of Genocide.* New York: Basic.

Solnit, Albert J. 1984. "Preparing." In *Psychoanalytic Study of the Child,* vol. 39, ed. Albert J. Solnit, Ruth S. Eissler, and Peter B. Neubauer, 613–32. New Haven: Yale University Press.

Wyman, David S. 1984. *The Abandonment of the Jews.* New York: Pantheon.